OUR LOVELY HOPS

MEMORIES OF HOP-PICKING IN KENT

EDITED BY PAM SCHWEITZER
WITH DIANNE HANCOCK

RESEARCH BY DIANNE HANCOCK AND PAM SCHWEITZER

PHOTOGRAPHY BY ALEX SCHWEITZER

TRANSCRIPTION BY JOHN SHERGOLD

DESIGN AND LAYOUT BY PAM AND ALEX SCHWEITZER

FOREWORD BY SAM WHITBREAD

Our lovely hops, our lovely hops,
When the measurer he comes round,
Pick 'em up, pick 'em up off the ground,
When he starts to measure,
He never knows when to stop,
Aye, aye jump in the bin
And take the bloomin' lot.

The painting on the front cover is entitled "Hop-picking on Whitbread's Hop Farm, 1937." It is by T. C. Dugdale, A.R.A., and was one of four paintings commissioned by Whitbreads from well-known artists of the day to hang in the bars of a thousand Whitbread public houses. This was the first occasion on which artists had been commissioned in this way, and in 1938, the four paintings were exhibited in the Royal Academy show, and were then reproduced by Whitbreads for members of the public to buy, priced 7/6 unframed or 21/- framed.

The painting on the back cover is by Rowland Hilder O.B.E. and was produced as a poster by Whitbreads circa 1950.

CONTENTS

CONTRIBUTORS

Ivy Arundale
Kathleen Ash
Marjorie Balcombe
Mary Baldwin
Tom Baldwin
Flo Batley
Bob Bennett
Marie Berry
Joyce Berry
Lola Berry
Albert Bowers
Florence Burgess
Lilian Carter
Joan Clarkson

Pat Davies
Harry Demarne
Bet Easterbrook
Tom Easterbrook
Anne Fitzgerald
Barbara Fitzgerald
Lilian Fitzgerald
Maureen Fitzgerald
Mike Fitzgerald
Charlotte Fowler
Hilary Irving
Alice Heskitt
Doug Hook
Bill Hudson

Elaine Jones
Ruby Jones
Leslie Kemp
Peg King
Vi Lewis
Minnie Martin
Joan Miller
Laura Murphy
Ethel Neighbour
Kit O'Connell
Frances O'Connell
Bill O'Sullivan
Eileen O'Sullivan
Joan Pearce

Alf Pharo
Vivien Prince
Stanley Rose
Ellen Russell
Dot Seadon
Jean Simmer
Bill Slack
Ellen Tucker
Rev. George Vince
Daphne Wallace
Bill Webb
Doris West
Tony Whytock
Mabel Wilson

Age Exchange wish to thank the following for their support with this project:

The staff of the Whitbread Hop Farm at Paddock Wood, the staff of the Cobtree Museum of Kent Life, Nick Redman
of the Whitbread Archive, David Wallace, Howard Bloch of Newham Local History Library,
Southwark Local History Collection, Tower Hamlets Local History Library.

The editors wish to thank Gwen Parrish for proof reading the manuscript, Sheila Robinson for helping on research,
Kit O'Connell for being our first guide into the hop-picking world and Anne Fitzgerald for a memorable hoppers' reunion.

Age Exchange are grateful to Thames/LWT Telethon for financial support with the allied Theatre in Education project on
hop-picking involving children, professional actors and older people at the Age Exchange Reminiscence Centre.

FOREWORD

The use of itinerant pickers for the English hop harvest is recorded as early as the beginning of the 18th century. As the hop acreage expanded so did the work force required to pick.

Londoners began to come down to Kent in the early 19th century, travelling at first on foot or by horse and cart. By 1900 thousands of Londoners were coming by rail every September to Kent where 40,000 acres were under hops for a month-long working holiday. 8,000 people came in "Hoppers' Specials" to Paddock Wood station alone from London Bridge.

In 1920 Whitbread acquired its well-known Hop Farm at Beltring, near Paddock Wood, where there were more than 750 huts with cookhouses, hot and cold water facilities and sanitation, together with shopping and recreational facilities. A hard day, in which some families picked up to 100 bushels of hops, was often followed by a sing-song round the fire.

At the end of the hop picking season Hop Supper Dances were given by farmers and Whitbread held their own Hop Festival, when an ox was roasted and the Hop Queen was crowned.

As a teenager I remember being taken to one of the last Beltring Hop Festivals in the early 1950s; after supper we were all entertained to a full-scale variety show with stars such as Billy Russell and David Nixon.

The need to reduce costs and increase farm productivity led in the 1950s to the introduction of hop-picking machinery which spelled the end of the annual migration of Londoners to the hop gardens of Kent. However, as this book vividly shows, the memories linger on and there are many Londoners today who look back with affection to the days when they went "down hopping, hopping down in Kent."

Sam Whitbread

Happy hoppers (photo lent by Kathleen Ash)

INTRODUCTION

"If you haven't been hopping, you haven't lived!" This was the general response of pensioners from the London area whose memories we sought for this publication. The vast majority look back on their childhood and adult hopping experience with enormous pleasure, and continue to miss those September trips which for many were the highlight of the year.

The more we asked questions, the clearer it became why people still hold their hopping memories so dear. They were glad to be able to leave over-crowded, ill-ventilated homes in smoke-filled dusty London where there was little open play area for the children. In an era when summer holidays were the exception rather than the rule, and where a day-trip to the sea-side was most people's annual excursion, Londoners felt privileged to be going for three or four weeks of fresh country air, out-door living, good food and above all for a special kind of camaraderie. "Down hopping", mothers and grandmothers, aunts and sisters could spend time pleasurably with each other and with the children from their extended families in an easy-going atmosphere with little noise and interruption. Children could be allowed to run free without fear of serious mishap, to spend time with their cousins and to get to know a wide range of new friends, often from different areas of London. There was every likelihood that these hopping friends would be there again the next year too, as families usually went back to the same farm for decades.

In most cases the women went hopping without their husbands, and for many this was an important temporary relief. For those with drinking husbands, it was a chance to escape from arguments and even violence, and to earn a bit of their own money to buy shoes and clothes for their children. For those whose husbands were in casual work connected with the Docks and related industries, where earnings were sporadic and insecurity was endemic, there was a reassuring certainty about their earnings from hop-picking. It was not a fortune, but the women could cover all the living expenses for them and their children, and still have a little left over. In many cases, the short absences made hearts grow fonder, so that many of the people we interviewed remembered the menfolks' weekend visits with particular pleasure. Where the men did stay in Kent with their wives or mothers, they were usually working alongside them in the fields as pole pullers (the men who cut down the bines for the women to pick into the bins) and this too was a very different working relationship from anything they had in London.

For a 1930s observer like George Orwell, whom we quote in these pages, the pleasures of hop-picking were far from obvious. His descriptions of the hard work, poor pay and appalling living conditions are completely at odds with the way the hop-pickers themselves remember the experience. It gives us some measure of the hard lives the women must have lived in London to be so appreciative of these few weeks in September. There is some evidence in these memories that the harshness of the hop-picking life took a bit of getting used to for people marrying into long-standing hopping families. Young brides were often told, "You're too fussy", and it must be said that plenty of people only went hopping once, their sharpest memories being of earwigs and scratchy straw bedding. Orwell's account might also suggest that memory is glamourising the hop-picking experiences in these accounts. However, the interviewees were unanimous in their reports of their pleasure and excitement on receiving their annual "hopping letter" from the farmer saying the family could go down to Kent and that there would be a hut waiting for them. For them the letter spelt three or four weeks of largely unalloyed pleasure, and they have no need to use rose-tinted glasses to look back on hopping.

Kentish people do not have comparably sunlit memories of the hop-picking season, but even they remember looking forward with excitement during August to the coming influx of Cockneys, and missing them in October when village life resumed its normal quiet slow rhythm. They observed the Londoners from afar as much as possible, using separate areas in the local pubs, fencing off the shop displays for fear of goods wandering, working in separate parts of the hop fields, and only rarely straying into the hut encampments. Londoners were an essential part of the local economy, and were useful people to blame when things went amiss or astray, but they remained a race apart for the "homedwellers".

In London too, hoppers were viewed askance by their neighbours. Hopping was something to look down on, almost a gypsy way of life, though the London hoppers in fact tended to keep themselves apart from the real gypsy pickers in Kent, except for occasional consultations on health matters. "Go down hopping, come back jumping" was a common saying, referring to what was perceived as a rough and dirty way of life. Children who returned late to school after a hopping holiday were taken straight to "Nitty Nora" for a thorough disinfection and delousing. All this disapproval is in stark opposition to the hoppers' own accounts of filling tin baths with hot water in difficult circumstances so that everyone could have a regular bath and hair wash. The idea of hopping being dirty and therefore unhealthy, is quite incomprehensible to the hoppers themselves, who felt that the fresh air gave them a far greater chance than their stay-at-home neighbours of health and welfare through the cold, smog-filled London winter ahead.

The passing of the hand-picking era was a matter of deep regret for all our interviewees. The arrival of machines spelt the end of free summer breaks for 50,000 Londoners. Those who continued to help out on mechanised farms soon abandoned the idea when they found that they were working indoors in the presence of noisy motors, doing the menial work of removing leaves, work which had often been left to children in the hand-picking days. In any case, the Londoners knew they were no longer needed, and had in fact been expecting mechanisation for some years before it hit their particular farm. Nevertheless, people cried when they were told that this would be their last year, and some older people just gave up the ghost, feeling they had nothing left to look forward to. Many Londoners continue to think of their hopping days now. We were told by older women that when they are browsing through the shops they find themselves saying, "Ooh that'd be handy down hopping", and have to pinch themselves to remember that they will not be going again.

This book is intended as a permanent record of the wonderful memories and photographs which we have been given by people from London and Kent. Their stories have been edited from taped interviews and grouped in chapters which we hope will give the reader a keen sense of the hop-picking season from start to finish. Age Exchange wishes to thank all the contributors for their stories, their time, their encouragement, their ideas and their enthusiasm. All of them are keen that younger people should know about hopping and its importance to so many Londoners. It was a vital ingredient in their lives when they were younger, and it is a treasured memory now.

Pam Schweitzer

Fresh air, fresh food for all the family (photo lent by Alf Pharo)

ESCAPE FROM LONDON

The women and the kids went hop-picking to earn a few coppers and to have a holiday really – it was the only holiday we had. We came from Bermondsey, where whole streets went hop-picking – it weren't just a question of a few: everybody in the street went. They used to leave behind the very old people and the men. The men used to stay behind because they were working in the docks. Dockers can look after themselves – they never went short of anything! They used to come down weekends on the Friday nights, and stay until Sunday night, and go back to work on Monday. To live in the country for three weeks, it was out of this world. Even though it was very primitive accommodation. I suppose we must have had our bad days, but I don't really remember. It was a great adventure being in the open all day with this tremendous amount of space to play in. I came from Bermondsey, and the streets were narrow and they smelt of the docks – wood and tar – not a bad smell, but the fresh air made you realise there were other things than the docks. Most of us finished up with chest troubles living in London but you only had to go out as far as Downham to get into the country.

Hopping was an era I think, it had to come and it had to pass; with modern ways, the old ways go.

Bill Webb

"All crammed into little streets."
(Greater London History Library)

My grandfather had a barrow down Hoxton market. He used to go down to the hop fields by lorry. All the stuff would be tied in bundles, no cases or anything like that, just tied up, bundled up. A lot of them used to pile on to a lorry, and take the old organ and the piano and everything else if they had the lorry. Everyone in those days had an upright piano in their front room, and all my dad's family had a natural ear. They sat down and played honkeytonk tunes, you know.

They always took the kids because it got them away to the fresh air, didn't it? It was a tonic for children. If you lived in a town, to take children away to the country for three or four weeks – well, the schools couldn't really have any objections, but it did mean the kids lost the first month of school every year.

Ellen Tucker

"Fresh air made you realise there were other things than the docks." (Southwark Local History Library)

My mother and grandmother were umbrella makers – working from home. They had started in that trade in 1915. My mother had four children and she used to take all of us hop-picking. Before the war, people went hop-picking to get their money; it was killing two birds with one stone. Apart from getting a holiday, they got paid for it as well. People in those days just couldn't afford a holiday. In those days you never had parks with much green in them. Where I lived we had two parks; one had no green at all. The other had a little bit of green but you weren't allowed to go on it. The only time I saw green grass was Easter time when we used to go to Blackheath Fair. We lived in Wapping. Most of the hopping people came from the East End. In 1936, my father said, "We'll go on holiday this year, we'll have a week at Ramsgate." The other people thought we were millionaires! After the war, people seemed to have more money. After the war you had men and women working, so you had more money, and you could afford a holiday.

Bob Bennett

Stepney stall holder (Tower Hamlets Local History Library)

I was born on 19 March 1910. That makes me eighty-one years old. And my family went hop-picking about fifteen times, that's fifteen years. In those days it was a holiday ... it was wonderful to get away from the home. We had a bad home life, my father was a drunkard. We were very poor, I had to go to school with no shoes on. I had to run through ice and frost. So anything was better than being at home. My mother used to take us hop-picking. It was a way of getting a few bob: we could come home and buy a new pair of shoes and have some decent food, that's how bad it was.

The 1930s were very, very bad; unemployment was rife, and you had the General Strike before that in 1926, and nobody had money. If somebody had a piano, they were rich. There were some families that were working, good luck to them, and they had a fair home. But ninety-nine per cent had nothing. They were very, very rough days. As soon as I was fourteen, I went into service as a page boy in a hotel. We couldn't afford to be kept at home; there wasn't any money. My mother used to go and sell bloody beetroot and mint to get a couple of pence. There were six of us in our family. Everyone was hard up. So you had to make your own entertainment, games, marbles in the street. Hop-picking was our only holiday. It was brilliant to get away from where we lived. But mind you, it was bloody hard down there, in the hop fields, but it was better there, because you had the open air. We used to play a game of football, or play cricket on Sundays in the fields, there were plenty of open places.

You could come home with two or three quid, which was a lot of money then. Now we're talking about the old days, and ha'pennies and pennies counted. And it could set you up for a little while, if you were down hop-picking for three or four weeks.

Stanley Rose

GENERATIONS OF HOPPERS

I was only about three months when I first went hop-picking. I was born in June, and by September I was hop-picking. That was something we did every year. We never did anything else, it was just our life. My mother and grandmother had gone hopping all their lives too. My grandmother's father died when she was young, and all her sisters were taken into service to earn a living. She was the only one left, so she and her mother used to go hop-picking just to earn money. By the time I got older, money was still important, but it wasn't the be-all and end-all. People just wanted to be there. It was the love of the life down there. It was so different in Kent from the life that we were used to in the East End. We were from Hoxton, which was a very, very poor area, all crammed into little streets. When we went hopping, we saw trees and fields and cows.

Elaine Jones

Pawn shop on a Monday morning
(Tower Hamlets Local History Library)

I came from Deptford, but my parents and grandparents came from the East End, Wapping and Stepney. My mother's mother and my father's mother were all hop-pickers since they were children. And my father's brothers – four of them – all went hop-picking every year, so we all met up there with their families. It's the only holiday they knew. Never knew their way to the seaside. I never saw the seaside until I married at twenty-one.

Marjorie Balcombe

When I first went hop-picking I used to go with my mother. There were seven of us in our family and my father worked in the docks. Fortunately he did have a regular job, which was unusual in the 1920s. He was a very good father and a good husband, he looked after us seven kids, but of course, we didn't get holidays. So it was grand for us to go hop-picking. You could be out all day, no school, lovely! Hop-picking, unfortunately, came about the end of August, when you had had your summer holidays and were ready to go back to school. Well, the schools didn't really take all that much notice if you took time off in those days, so we were all able to go. Until I went to a Central school and then of course I couldn't go hop-picking, because you couldn't leave that school to go. You'd have been in trouble. All my brothers and sisters used to go and I had to stay with my grandmother and grandfather.

My mother used to go hop-picking with her mother. But after she got married, my father didn't like the idea very much at all. Still, once the children starting coming along, they came a bit thick and fast and then he didn't mind the idea of hop-picking so much! Really it was for the best because they had a holiday, my Mum had a change, and she earned some money. It never was a lot of money, but it seemed like a fortune. It helped you to get the Christmas things.

Whitbread's had more modern technology than the smaller farms. They did have horsedrawn wagons that used to bring the hops back from the fields, but on the whole, they were far more mechanised. They were in advance of everywhere else. They employed far more people and they had more fields to pick. Even in those days, we had hot water and showers – primitive ones, I suppose, but they were lovely. They used to have one night for the women, and one night for the men and the next night for the women, and then a night for the men and so on. I must give it to Whitbread's, because they really were ahead of their time. It was difficult to get on to a Whitbread farm, usually it was handed down within families. I would say at least three generations of my family before me picked at Whitbread's – before that, I can't say but my mother and my grandmother and her mother definitely went. It wasn't called Whitbread's then. I think it was called White's Farm. I went back there a little while ago and it's a museum now. Actually, there are pictures of me in there, picking at the bin, in one of the oast houses they've converted for the museum.

Kathleen Ash

GIVING UP WORK FOR HOPPING

I started work at fourteen in dressmaking, learning to sew, everything done by hand, buttonholes, hems, everything. But I had to give up my job in September because the family went hop-picking and my father wouldn't leave me behind – I had to go as well. I would have liked to have been a grown-up and stayed at home on my own. But then everyone else had gone, so there was no question of my being left behind. And once I was down there, of course I liked it.

When I got back to London, I decided I would go into clerical work instead. They wouldn't give you a paid holiday, so I still used to lose my job every year because father insisted I go hop-picking. You'd try and get the same job back, but they'd always given it to someone else. Still, this was just after the war, and you could walk in and out of firms. There was no problem finding another job.

When I met my husband, he'd never been hop-picking, and I introduced him to the hop field. We started going for our summer holidays. And then when I got married and my daughter was in a pushchair still, a little girl used to come round and take her out for walks and that. I took her and we went down with the family, and I had my own hut and my own bin for the first time ever. I was about twenty then. I was a bit worried at first, but we did quite well actually. I earned more money in that two weeks than I would have at home. We paid our way, we had the air and the holiday. The girl I took with me, she went home with a few pounds in her pocket as well.

Ellen Tucker

Anne Fitzgerald's mum gave up her tailoring job to go hopping.

Mum was a tailoress, and always had work, so we were never really poor. But she used to give her job up to go. It was just the atmosphere that was really lovely. Everybody did it. If the women were working they used to give their job up.

Anne Fitzgerald

You wasn't supposed to say anything about going hopping at school but if you weren't there at the beginning of term, the teacher would say, "Have you been hop-picking?" "No, Miss." But I think the colour of you give the game away. You'd be burnt from the sun. Loads of people were missing at the start of term, you'd know that they were hop-picking.

I actually went on to a grammar school so I had to come home during the week and then go back on Friday night until Sunday. My dad stayed at home with me, because he had to work. He'd go back down to Kent on the Friday. And that's how it all worked really. But I hated it when I had to stay at home. Everybody was having a good time, hop-picking. I don't think that lasted too long before I decided to take off all the hop-picking time.

Elaine Jones

I was twelve when I first went hop-picking. I was the eldest one of the family. I met a friend and I said to her where did she go for a holiday, and she said "hop-picking". So I came home and told my mum, "Annie Stork's going hopping and she said can I go with her?" "You ask Annie Stork where she's going – if they go, we can go!" That's the first time Mum had ever been hop-picking in her life. We loved it!

When I was in service, Mum used to say, "Don't forget to tell the lady, you've got to have the last week in August and the first week in September for your holiday" so I could go hop-picking with her. Well I went into one job and asked for my two weeks' leave and she said no, I'd have to have my holiday while they were away; and Mum said, it doesn't matter when they go away, you've got to have it when I want you to have it! Because I'd been in service, to go away hopping, it was freedom! It was a lovely atmosphere down there every year.

Laura Murphy

My first memories of hop-picking were of when we got our letter from the farmer saying the hops were ready to pick. This was in the East End of London. The majority of people down the street where I lived went hop-picking at the same time and on the same farms as us. My dad and my elder brothers used to stay in the house in London during that time because they were at work there.

We always knew what farm we were going to. My mum had been going there for twenty years. The farmer used to send you a card saying how many people they would accept. If you were a good family and you picked well he would have you every year. If there were any men out of work, on the labour, they used to ask if they could come hop-picking with us, and my mum used to say, "Yes, you can come, but you'll have to work. If you don't work you don't eat." So she used to have two or three chaps hanging around unemployed. All the farmers wanted us because we were good workers. Some farmers didn't have so long picking as others, so when we had finished at one farm, we used to go on to another. We took all our gear from the first farm on to the next.

Years ago we would have been down there five to six weeks hop-picking. We all started hop-picking on the first of September. Whichever farm it was, we always started on the first of September and then we'd go right through to the middle of October. The school terms were just the same as now, so we'd just have to miss six weeks of school. In fact, we missed more than that in my family, because we used to go hop-training in May. That's when the hops begin to grow and you have to twist them round the strings. Then we used to go fruit-picking at Vincent's farm in Wateringbury and then on to another farm hop-picking. So we used to spend about six months down there really: May, June, July, August, September and October.

When we got back to London and we'd been hop-picking and missed all that time from school, the other kids used to be quite envious because we were brown and had all new clothes. It was terrific. We were the aristocrats of the school. We used to take home great big hopping apples. It was dishonest but probably expected. You'd proabably go and pinch a chicken or two to bring home and a bag of potatoes and cabbages and whatever.

Kit O'Connell

After the war up until the 1960s, I worked at the Evelina Children's Hospital, Southwark. Hop-picking was an annual event which caused a lot of excitement. It was a chance to get away from the overcrowded streets and bad living conditions in Southwark. On my way to the Hospital from London Bridge, I would hear loud laughter and shouting – turn a corner and find at least one lorry being packed up with household goods, chairs, cases, pots, pans, etc. They were going down to the hop fields in Kent. Children would be agog with excitement and parents would shout threatening remarks to them as they got in the way of the packing up. Bedding would be thrown out of windows to be loaded onto the cart below – everything but "the kitchen sink" would be packed up for the long journey down the Old Kent Road, maybe over Blackheath and down the roads to the hop fields.

From time to time, "casualties" would arrive back at our hospital. A child would return with an arm or a leg in plaster – often from falling out of a tree when scrumping. During a wet summer, we'd get a child with a chest infection or tummy bug from eating too much fruit, or maybe a skin rash from the bines themselves. Anyway, the fun of it all seemed to far outweigh the mishaps of three weeks' hopping in September.

Vivian Prince

We used to do hop-picking *and* fruit-picking. We'd leave London in May, and come back about the second week in October. We'd do the fruit-picking at Wateringbury, then straight on through to the hop-picking at Mill Pond Farm. The whole family would go. Mum and Dad, seven of us children, my aunt and my uncle, my other aunt and uncle, Nan and Granddad. We'd go down about the last week in May to get the huts washed, white-washed and ready for the season's picking. My father and my uncle used to work for a brewery firm and the firm used to let them have the lorry for a weekend, so Mum could come down with the furniture, blankets, pots and pans for the huts. There was a place at Sellinge, when I was a kid, it had a thousand hop huts on one common – where the huts were, you'd call it "a common". A thousand huts on one common. A thousand families at hop-picking time.

Albert Bowers

The Bowers family by their hop hut.

I was country born, born in Hampshire, so hop-picking didn't come strange to me, it was country life. My father died, and we had no means of living so we had to move from Hampshire to Silvertown in London. But each year, we would go hop-picking down to Five Oak Green. The local greengrocer used to use his lorry to take everybody down with their bits and bobs. You all used to pile into the back of his van. We used to go to the same farm each year, so our same hut was there waiting for us! The picking used to last about a month, sometimes it ran over, but normally a month it was. That used to pay for our new winter clothes.

Pat Davies

My gran, Martha Perry, was a terrific character. She was very fat and she was about four foot ten. She had little short fat fingers, my nan. She hated the stuff dropping on her head, so she always wore a scarf. She didn't like the sun on her, so invariably she wore a jumper of some sort with a great big apron over it. Under that she would wear a cloth purse, like a butcher's pocket with her money in. She's sitting on the side of the bin.

Joan Clarkson

TAR BABIES

We went hop-picking every year. My mum wouldn't have missed going for the world, she loved it. There was ten of us, and I was the fifth; five girls and five boys. That was our annual holiday and we'd gone every year since we were children, except when we were more grown up and courting. We wouldn't always want to go then. We always had the same hut at Wheeler's Farm at Claygate, Marden. They kept it for my mum, special. She used to take curtains and divide it off into different rooms.

I went every year from when I was a little girl. Even when I was working, I'd go down at weekends. When I had my own children I took them hopping too. One year when my first two were still little, I decided not to go because they had had whooping cough and the doctor said I should take them somewhere where they were using tar. That was supposed to be good for chests. My mum said, "Why don't you bring them down hopping? They're tarring round the edge of the field." So I took them down there. Well, I'm busy picking on these bins, when all of a sudden they come up to me holding hands and they was covered from head to foot with tar. They said "We fell in the tar." Well, I took them to the Red Cross hut where there was a nurse, and we had to cut their hair off and wash them. They got better anyway, and now they're grown up with their own children and grandchildren. So the tar worked!

Florence Burgess

Father only allowed us to go hop-picking because I was a frail child and I'd been very ill. My mother had already lost a child and she had almost had a breakdown. My brother was fifteen months old when he died. He'd had pneumonia three times, and measles. Mother never talked about it. She never made any fuss, she never ever spoke about my brother, but in fact she never really recovered. I was seven the first time I remember going.

There was my gran, my mum's younger sister and her two younger brothers. There was my sister and me and my mother. My gran's children were the same age as my older sister. My mother was the eldest of the family. You know they had children for many years then, my grandmother had nine children. And my mother being the oldest, we grew up with the youngest! It wasn't unusual to grow up with aunts and uncles of your own generation.

So you always had a community life, a lot of family life going on around you. You were always very involved. Someone was getting married, someone was having babies.

The second year that I remember going, 1938, my father's brother died. He was only thirty five, and he'd left four children, three girls and a little baby boy, so my mother took the three girls hopping. That meant she had five of us to look after, but she just made one big bed upstairs, and we all slept in it, and my mother slept on the outside, in any sort of room that was left! People did just put children all in together, and as we were all girls it didn't make a lot of difference.

My father didn't like to rough it. He would come down to bring my mother her housekeeping money every Sunday. That meant she didn't really have to work. She only picked because she wanted to take us away as it was good for us, built us up. It was a working holiday, and most people there needed the money and had to pick, but my sister and I were very lucky. We didn't have to pick hops if we didn't want to. We roamed the fields, we went scrumping, blackberry-picking – very naughty! We always had a lot of freedom there which we didn't have at home. We were allowed to go out with the local children, really just joining in with anything that was going on. As long as my mother knew where we were, she didn't worry.

Joan Clarkson

PREPARATIONS FOR HOPPING

THE LETTER

You used to have to wait for your letter to arrive before you could go hopping. Until you got your letter, you didn't know you were going to be allowed to go. We used to go down with my gran. For her, it was a way of life; you got away from everything for four or five weeks. Lots of grandmothers took their grandchildren. We used to wait for her to get her letter from Whitbreads. Every day through the school holidays I used to drive her mad, "Have you got your letter, Nan, have you got your letter?"

Joan Clarkson

You had to write in to the farmer round about April, May and tell him what bins you wanted, and then if they'd got them, they'd write and tell you, "Have reserved you so many bins." That's when you started getting your bits and pieces together, your pots and pans and everything. You got your stuff together gradually through the year, wellingtons, and clothes for the kids so they can go about any-old-how, sort of thing, because it's no good putting good clothes on them while they're picking hops.

They used to go from all over London: Elephant and Castle, Hackney, Hoxton, all the way round. You always used to meet up with them once a year. And of course the kids would have grown up a bit every year. It was fascinating. Our kids used to look forward to it. They had some really good times. That was their holiday. We couldn't afford a holiday otherwise.

Ellen Russell

When you wrote to Mr Dawes, the farmer, you'd say, "We had hut so-and-so last year." I don't know whether Mr Dawes said she could have it, or whether Mum was just lucky enough to get the same one when we went down the following year. Sometimes it would be: "Ooh, that's my hut, you shouldn't be in there, because that's our hut." Once you knew it was your hut, it was, "Well, we're going up to Dawesy, we'll soon clear it up, soon settle that." People got out then, because they knew it was your hut. If Dad had put shelves up one year, when we went down the next year the shelves would still be up. Sometimes you'd paper the hut. It was whitewashed. Dad used to come down sometimes and put up wall paper, so it was really posh, dear, really posh!!

Laura Murphy

Around the end of August, people would all be asking one another, "You got your letter yet?" Because they got their letter to say when they would start picking the hops. "Have you got your letter? So and so's got her letter – we haven't got ours yet!" It was quite exciting because in them days, people didn't receive many letters, because they were poor. But at this one time of year, all these brown envelopes would arrive. So they used to know that the brown envelope was their hop-picking letter. "Have you got your letter? Have you got your brown envelope?" That was the beginning, that was the exciting part. People were worried about if they were going to get their letter!

Bill O'Sullivan

We used to get this card to say we could go hopping, and we used to meet Mrs Smith, Mrs Jones, Mrs White, "I've got my hop-picking card!" We were all running up and down, all lots and lots of excitement, waving this card. "We'll see you there."

When the children were returning to school, we used to go off hop-picking. Well everybody was in the same boat, half the school was gone; they'd all gone hop-picking. The school board never used to like it because we'd already had our seven weeks holiday, but they couldn't do nothing about it.

Marjorie Balcombe

If you wanted to go hop-picking for the first time, you'd write to the farmer beforehand. And then you'd wait until he'd replied. If there was a vacancy, depending on how many pickers he needed that year, you'd get a reply. If someone had died since the last hop-picking time, there would be space for a new picker. The new pickers would go and they'd have the huts that were left. If you didn't get no letter, there was no point in going. So you waited for your letter so you'd know that your place was booked. It was like a booking really.

I was a baby when I first went hopping. I can remember my mother always telling the story about when she was taking me to the shops in a pram and she got her hopping money in a purse. She gave the purse to me to play with in the pram, and I threw the purse out of the pram. When she got to the shops she'd got no money. Nobody had any money in those days – you waited until the end of the week and you subbed on the money you'd been earning the week before.

Eileen O'Sullivan

STYLE & WINCH, Ltd.

PHONE: HUNTON 85132.

MANAGER:
E. H. BURR.

BUSTON MANOR FARM,
HUNTON,
NR. MAIDSTONE.

HOP-PICKING, 1946.

Working hours this year will be governed by Siren, and will be as follows :—
8.0 a.m. till 12.0 noon and from 1.0 p.m. till 5.0. p.m.

Particular attention is called to this Rule and Pickers who feel they cannot keep to these times are strongly advised not to sign attached card as this Rule will be strictly adhered to.

No bin may be occupied by less than two adult pickers, *viz.*: by persons of 16 years of age or over, and rail fares will be paid on this number only.

Children under 14 years of age will be allowed to pick, but will not be regarded as pickers by the management for any purpose whatever

In all cases of time-keeping, due consideration will be given to sick and infirm persons, but a local doctor's or nurse's certificate will be required.

Bins left unoccupied for more than one complete working day will be removed from the gardens, and the account closed, unless a satisfactory explanation is left at the main office, such as cases of hardship.

No accommodation will be provided for non-pickers, and any persons found occupying a picker's dwelling without permission will be proceeded against for trespass.

A deposit of 5/- will be charged for loan of lock and key, and this amount will be refunded if returned in good condition upon completion of picking.

The enclosed card must be returned within fourteen days.

STYLE & WINCH, LTD.

One Bin.
Hur. 85.
Drift 2.

THE HOPPING BOX

Weeks and weeks before we went hop-picking, my mum would go shopping and she'd get a tin of milk, a tin of beans or something like that and put that away in a box. She'd keep doing that so by the time you came to go down to Kent, you had a boxful of tins and that, all ready to start.

Charlotte Fowler

My mother-in-law used to have a space out in the garden and every time she went out shopping, she used to put something away for the hop-picking cart. Tins of stuff. So when hopping time came round, she had her larder full up.

Vi Lewis

My mum would go to the second-hand stall and buy all second-hand clothes for us to wear. You had to have so many old clothes, especially if it was raining. You had to keep changing, so you needed extra, plus we were already very poor, so it didn't matter to us that we had second-hand. We would take pots and pans and all our clothes and bedding, lino, wallpaper, a bag of flour to do the hut out when we got there. We put all our luggage in the pram and pushed it to London Bridge Station. Then we were off.

Kit O'Connell

My grandmother had what she called her hopping box. It was a large wooden box on wheels. She'd had it built specially. It was as big as a chest, with a lid, but on wheels so that it was easy to push and manoeuvre about. Being a widow on her own, she couldn't manage too many cases and bags. Into that box she used to pack her linen for the bed, her clothes and woollies, a beautiful oil lamp and her books to read. My gran always read.

Joan Clarkson

People that went hop-picking from year to year would take the same things with them so they wouldn't be used from one year to the next. You'd keep them out in the shed ready for the next hop-picking. When you came home, all the linen, the mattress covers and the pillow cases would be boiled and washed and everything would be packed away.

Laura Murphy

My husband made a big wooden box with wheels on it for all our goods, and bedding and food. You'd take your supplies down with you. He made it like a cabinet, with two doors and a leaf, so that when you pulled the doors out you could make a proper table out of it. I remember the doors and the padlock. It was about as big as a tea chest.

Ethel Neighbour

Before we went down hopping, Dad used to make a new rag mat for the living room, so we could take the old one to the hop huts. He used to make them from odd bits of rags, bits of old blanket, old coats and trousers, anything. He used to cut the pieces up, dye them and he would make patterns, maybe diamond shapes, in red and black. Last year's rag rug would go to the hop hut to be put at the end of our bed.

Laura Murphy

THE JOURNEY TO KENT

We used to go hop-picking from Deptford, right from when I was born. I think I went down there in a pram. My older brother is three years older than me and my younger brother is two years younger. And we were always together the three of us and we never separated at all. They always had it drummed into them they had to take care of me.

We had to walk from Abinger Grove in Deptford to New Cross Gate station. My father made a wooden box, and he bought some pram wheels second-hand from a stall in Deptford. He fixed these pram wheels under the box and a handle on it. That was the one box we had all our luggage in. We used to take our cups from home. We only had five cups, no spare; so you packed those cups in the box overnight, and when we wanted a cup of tea in the morning before we left, we had them in jam jars, we were that hard up. We also had a tin trunk that had been in my family for years. It was my grandma's, and it had been all the colours of the rainbow. Everybody used to paint it blue, green, black, white, whatever. This tin trunk would be tied on top of the wooden box and we had to push it on its wheels to New Cross Gate and we caught the four o'clock train in the morning down to Marden.

When we got to New Cross Gate, we couldn't afford to pay the fare so we were lifted over the wall. And we knew exactly where to cross the lines to be safe. My father used to take my older brother with him and my mother. He had to push the luggage through the ticket barrier, but prior to that he lifted me and my other younger brother, Alf, over the wall. So Alf took care of me, crossed the lines, got to the other platform. So we got through. And when we got on the train, until it left the station, we were pushed under the seat out of the way so we wasn't seen. No-one was ever caught. I think they knew. You see it wasn't only us; all the Old Kent Road people, all the Deptford people, the New Cross area, if you'd got three or four children you couldn't afford the fare for all of them. People would be taking their cats with them, and take the budgie, take the dog on a lead or in a box or in your bag. No-one to look after them in London, so the cat's taken.

Marjorie Balcombe

We lived in London, not far from London Bridge station – where we travelled from down to the hop fields. We'd put all our things on a barrow and get the men to push the barrow to the station. When you got to the station, they'd pack all the things into the van on the train and then you'd find your coach and sit down. When you got to the place, the trouble you'd have finding anything! "Oh where's my pots? Where's my pans?"

Dot Seadon

We used to catch the hop-pickers' train at three o'clock in the morning. There would be people from all areas: Stepney, Bermondsey, nearly everyone went off. There weren't many people in those areas who didn't go off hop-picking. One year, when I was quite small, my mum didn't have enough money for train fare for all of us, so she only got a ticket for herself and two halves. A couple of us were put in empty sacks and put on the luggage racks. Unfortunately for my mum the inspector decided to investigate and one of us had our feet showing. He let my mum off and said that he had never seen a sack with feet before.

My family all used to travel down in the same compartment. We were all ages – some were getting married, but they'd still come hop-picking. I think there were about thirty of us and we used to have about five huts between us.

Kit O'Connell

15

I've been hop-picking since I was a child. All my mother's people went to Lily Farm in Tonbridge: father, brother, sisters, so we went there too. My father used to carry his bundle to London Bridge station, and us kids used to carry these bags, hopping pots and all what we had. We walked from Spitalfields to London Bridge. There was a big open space at London Bridge and all the hoppers' stuff was stacked against the wall, bundles and kids akip, donkey carts, hand barrows, prams. We used to get up there about quarter to twelve.

It was two bob on the hoppers' train. You had two coppers on the gate, and two porters. Show your tickets as you go through the gate, "Right, away you go, 'way you go."

One year, when I was about ten, my oldest brother and his friend were going hopping and they decided to take me with them as their skivvy, to look after their hut. I had my hair cut first thing, they took the lot right off. Bald headed I was. And they got an old dog with them called Spot, took him and all. They didn't want to leave him behind. They pushed us through the ticket barriers, no tickets, and we gets on the train, not the corridor trains, just the single compartment trains. We was sitting there all sides when the ticket bloke comes along for the tickets. They shoved me under the seat with the dog, and those two were sitting there. The dog is quiet enough. He's heard the ticket bloke come along, "Tickets! Tickets!" He goes, "Grrrr." Course that was right against my head, I had my head to him. When they got me out I cried my eyes out.

Mike Fitzgerald

You'd march up to London Bridge about three o'clock in the morning. And then you'd get on a train – you used to wait there for hours and hours before the train went, and it used to take you down to the place where you'd go and pick the hops. There was a main station, such as Marden or Paddock Wood, and then you'd wait there. The farmer would send his cart down to the station to pick you up, and take you back to the farm.

Ellen Russell

They used to get somebody to take all the luggage up to London Bridge in a horse and cart. Then they would get on the train and they got up to all the tricks to save a copper or two. They'd take one or two of the children to carry big parcels for them, and they'd say to the guard, "Well they're only going to put those down for me." And sometimes the women would walk through the barrier with one of the youngest hidden in the long skirts they used to have.

Harry Demarne

It wasn't until the last week in August or the first or second week in September, that we'd all go up to London Bridge from Bermondsey. About the end of August, they would all start buying and storing their pots and different things. They used to make a box, a big box with two handles and four wheels. It used to have a lift up lid on it. They used to pack everything inside that and lock it down, put a lock on it. It looked like a shopping trolley, but much bigger. They used to push that cart from the Docklands up to London Bridge Station.

There were special trains for the hop-pickers and they were always very early in the morning, about four o'clock in the morning. They'd put all the luggage in the guards van, pile it up! In them days, everybody helped everybody else, because we were all children with our mothers and fathers. There were six in my family, three girls and three boys, so we all helped out.

Bill O'Sullivan

My father used to work on the railway and used to come down to hop-picking on his privileged ticket that took him and my mother. But there were six of us kids! So four of us had to hide under the seats and two were paid for. The ticket man would come round and mark the tickets and then the kids used to come out from under the seats after he'd gone. When the train stopped in one of the stations, the ticket inspector would get on and all the kids would disappear. It was like a telephone down the train. He'd jump in number one carriage, and the kids would be looking out the window. They'd call out "He's getting in number two now!"

Bill O'Sullivan

I first went hop-picking in 1909 as a five-month old baby in "long clothes", as my mother used to tell me. I went every year till 1939 and then after the war I went to Matfield until about 1950. Even after that, we always had a charabanc outing or later a car trip down to the hop fields until the '60s.

When I was a very young boy, my dad used to try to dodge the train fare for me. I had to hide under the seat when the inspector got on to clip the tickets. At Horsemonden, my dad hid me in a sack, put me over his shoulder, and got past the ticket collector. Then disaster! The bottom fell out of the sack, I got a cracked head, and my dad still had to pay the fare for me.

Tom Baldwin

HOP-PICKING STARTS KENT NEXT WEEK.

———— ◆ ————

SPECIAL TRAINS TO CARRY 60,000 PICKERS.

————

Hop-pickers arriving in Kent (photo lent by John Wardley)

A RAILWAY GUARD REMEMBERS THE HOPPER TRAINS

I was a railway guard, and hopping was always considered a spare job, because it wasn't part of the usual routine. All the rolling stock that they used for the hopping trains was very ancient and it was kept at South Bermondsey, Brick Layers Arms. It was kept in special sheds down there, and it was just not touched from year to year, as it was only really used for hopping. It was our job to get it out from there and bring it up the Smoke. You reversed your engine round as you went into London Bridge, Low Level, at platform eight and nine, and there you had all your hoppers waiting.

Most of them had gone and got their tickets a couple of days beforehand. You'd see them queuing at London Bridge. It was slightly cheaper for them. They put on extra ticket inspectors at the station so they'd probably be pretty alert, but then London Bridge was easy to get on because you could come across the footway over the top from other platforms and get down to where the hopping trains went from, so you didn't have to go past the barrier.

Often we'd actually got the trains into the platform before they got there, but occasionally you had problems getting in, and the hoppers were already on the platform. Quite a sight to behold. The people had come up from places like Stratford, West Ham, and some of them had pushed prams all the way up from Canning Town and right the way over, over the bridge. They were family groups going, I should say about seven or eight. There were often people late for the train, running, and things dropping off. It was amazing what they actually took down with them. You expected bedding and that, but I can remember clocks dropping, not grandfather clocks, but quite large clocks. It really was a sight to see. A lot of them'd just have the old galvanised baths they used for the wash on the Friday night, and that was filled up with all their stuff, and one held one handle and one the other.

We used to have extra vans, called PMV vans, put on the back of the train, just to take all their bulky stuff. You allowed plenty of time for everybody to get all their belongings on board and then they'd all pile in these compartments just as if it was a day out at the seaside.

There were one or two corridor trains, but the majority weren't, so you couldn't get any ticket inspection on the trains. There was usually a ticket inspection at the terminal station, but I don't think they tried all that hard anyhow to stop them. The train was only going to places like Paddock Wood, and terminated there. The journey took about an hour and a quarter I would say. They're far faster than that today, but then it was all steam trains. They'd often stop at New Cross or New Cross Gate to pick people up.

I remember once going down on the Hastings line, and in those days the tunnels would only take certain stock. You had to have special rolling stock to get through. Nobody thought to check the hopper train and they were so old they had chimney pots on top to let the air in. But when it came along to the tunnel it knocked all of these chimney pots flat. And that was the hoppers' train.

When we got to Paddock Wood or Yalding, we unloaded it all, and they'd be picked up from there. One or two you'd see just trudging off down the road, walking to the hop fields.

And then we would put the same trains on at a certain date to bring them back from hopping. There wouldn't be that much variation each year, just a week or so depending on when it was finished. In fact, I think there must have been set dates for going and returning, because we had our schedules all printed out and handed out to us weeks before the actual hopping. A lot of them didn't come back with us anyhow, as they made their own way back. Their final pay-off usually went straight in the pubs. They did a roaring trade in that area.

Doug Hook

LURE OF THE HOP.

BEGINNING OF THE GREAT TREK.

The annual exodus of prospective hoppers to the fields of Kent began modestly some days ago, but the flow is gradually increasing, and will reach its maximum before many days are over. Last week the majority of early season hoppers were travelling by road—motor lorries being the most favoured vehicle.

The long recent spell of unsettled weather is looked upon by old hands as a hopeful sign. They prophecy that it is likely to be followed by an equally long period of quiet sunny weather of the "sweet September" type—in fact the more optimistic ones would not be at all surprised if we experienced what is known as an Indian summer during two or three weeks of that month.

The hops are of very good quality this year, but the quantity is said to be below the average. Some of the experienced hoppickers earn as much as 10s. or 12s. a day —when weather permits.

Bermondsey Bills' Opinions.

" 'Oppin's all right when the wevver's right " a rather weedy Bermondsey young man, pushing a barrow-load of hopper's impedimenta, explained to a " Recorder " representative in Jamaica Road on Tuesday. " The smell o' the 'ops makes us 'ungry as 'unters, and the scenery arahnd Kent is lovely, not 'arf it aint ! Me and the missus allus eats and drinks twice as much when we're pickin' than we does sittin' at 'ome 'ere dahn among the pickle factories and railway arches ; and don't we git brahn wiv the sun ! It's a jolly good holiday, not arf. Lot better than the Bun Factory.

" Well, that's right enough, guv'nor, what you sez : its only a 'oliday when the sun's out. When it don't shine and it rains 'eavens 'ard for a day or two right off like it does some seasons, it's misery a'settin' there in our wooden sheds, lookin' aht at it a-comin' dahn like cats an' dawgs, and wishin' we 'adn't come 'oppin'. P'raps there's kids sqallin' rahnd us, and the floor gits into a nawful state of wet and mud. 'Ow we does long at such times for the pubs and the pictures and fried fish shops of good old Bermondsey and Rotherhithe !

" Still, it aint allus as bad as that, thank Gawd, and when the sun comes out agin we forgits all our little troubles and think o' what good times we'll 'ave when we gits back agin to Bermondsey, with a pocketful o' ooftish.

" Well, so long, guv'nor. I'm just going to 'ave one and then off we goes by train with out little lot. So long ! "

We used to talk about going hopping all the year round, and we used to look forward to going. We used to wait for the day to arrive when we would go to London Bridge station, although it was four o'clock in the morning! We'd all queue up with our boxes all the way up to London Bridge station, waiting for the train to get onto the platform. We could be waiting there for two hours until the train came. It was all steam trains then. They used to let us in and open the guard's van doors, and put all the cases and boxes in and then off we'd go!

Bill O'Sullivan

There were special hop-picking trains that were cheap rate. When you went by train, you had to pack everything up. People made boxes on wheels, or packed things in prams, if you could get a pram. Sometimes you'd walk from the station. Whitbread's had big Shire horses that used to pull the poke carts. They used to send these wagons up to the station to meet the hop-picking trains. And you could put your luggage on there and get a lift down to the farm.

Kathleen Ash

We'd go Paddock Wood. We'd be met there by the farmer's wagon. He'd say, "You going to Wheelers Farm?" and we'd all get in the cart. People knew the wagon driver, they went year after year. It was like a family, we knew everybody from the year before. We would get on the wagon with all our belongings and clip clop down to the farm. Sometimes, the men would walk and the women, children and boxes would be put on the wagon. Or the man would wheel the hopping box to the farm.

Bill O'Sullivan

And then when we got off at Marden, the farmer used to say, "Right, you've got wheels so you can push your luggage. We'll take the trunks, but you can push your boxes." And there was a lot with wheels. We travelled to the farm in the farmer's hay wagon sitting on the luggage. He'd take the women and children. My mother and I got a ride on the wagon, while my brothers wheeled the box two miles to the farm. It was like an army of hop-pickers. And some of them were real oh-gor-blimeys! Every other word was, f..., or bloody, or this, that and the other. We weren't, although father came from that area, I've never heard him swear or anything like that.

Marjorie Balcombe

We used to go hop-picking to a place called Boughton, and that was on the way to Canterbury, between Faversham and Canterbury. You'd have the lorry to pick you up from London. You decided you wanted to go down hopping, and you found somebody who was driving down there. Or you might meet someone who'd say, "We're going off hop-picking!" And then you'd say, "Oh, what about us?" Normally, they'd allocate one woman to be the governor, to make the arrangements for the lorry. It might be a big furniture van, or open van. You'd pack all your stuff in; you'd take old clothes, well, all you had was old clothes in those days, no good stuff. Always take some sort of mac, because you had to pick even if it rained, or you'd get no money. We had nothing else to take *but* our old clothes! We were on what they called the RO, that was the Relieving Officer – you'd call it Social Security now.

The lorry would be there waiting in the morning. You put all your luggage on there and away you'd go. And when the lorry got to Chatham Hill, the men would have to get off and push the blooming thing up the hill, to relieve their weight. Too heavy! But who cares, it got us there!

Stanley Rose

18

We used to hire a van, there'd be about seven of us. The van would carry all the gear, and the bedding, cups and saucers, pans, everything we'd required; it was like moving house for a few weeks.

Bill Webb

My job the rest of the year was on the meat transport, heavy transport goods. I'd take meat from Smithfield Market and take it off right over the country. So I did a lot of driving. I had this lorry I was driving, and when hopping came, I used to take the whole lot down in one go, all their luggage, in a five ton Bedford. Used to pick them all up from Hoxton, St. Lukes, Stepney, Wapping, Deptford Green, all that. Pick them all up. Charge them a bob, leave at about eleven o'clock and get down to Tonbridge about one. For hop-picking I'd probably have a fortnight's holiday. Well I was a pole puller, but I'd class it as a holiday. Even then, I was always out driving, taking the fellows down there at weekends or taking hoppers to Tonbridge to get their groceries, and pick them up.

Mike Fitzgerald

The local greengrocer had a big lorry and he used to take us down to the hop fields in that. We used to take a big tea chest with all our clothes in it. You would put all your stuff in the lorry, get in, up with the old tailboard, and away you went. A lot of hop-pickers went down by train. We never did, we always went by lorry.

Bob Bennett

If you went by train you used to get down the farms about half past four! There'd be a train load and when you got to the other end, the farmer used to be there with his cart to pick you up and all your luggage.

Vi Lewis

HOPS LURING VAST ARMY TO KENT

This Week-End Sees Start Of Great Invasion

5,000 Converging On Paddock Wood

BY road and rail the vast army of hop-pickers which annually invades Kent, will be converging towards the county this week-end.

Advance parties are, in many centres, "in residence," and picking starts in earnest early next week.

It was decided to start picking at Messrs. Whitbread's and several other farms in the Tonbridge area and the Weald this Friday.

At Paddock Wood, where arrangements are complete for the housing of 5,000 pickers, Messrs. Whitbreads have introduced more innovations.

Hops everywhere are of good size and stated to be of exceptional quality.

Babies Will Have A Big Show

PICKING will have begun by to-day most probably at East Peckham, Beltring, Yalding and Marden.

Generally, however, a big start will not be made until the beginning of next week.

On Thursday several special trains carried hundreds of hop-pickers to Paddock Wood.

By the end of this week a large proportion of the huge army of hop-pickers from London which annually invades Paddock Wood and other parts of the Weald will have arrived.

"ARISTOCRATS" BY TAXI

Most come by train and bus; others on bicycles and on foot; while in a few cases the "aristocrats" of the hop gardens will have followed their usual custom and travelled by taxi, intent on a holiday which pays for itself.

Earlier in the week at Messrs. Whitbread's, Paddock Wood, where thousands are employed, no decision had been made as to whether work should start this week-end or on Monday. It was felt, however, that the first bine should be pulled before the week-end if possible.

Kent Messenger, August 28th 1937

Arriving in style at the hop fields 1930s (photo lent by John Wardley)

SETTLING IN

Arriving at Paddock Wood station, awaiting collection by farm wagons (photo lent by Whitbread Hop Farm)

REUNION

When you met up with the other hoppers, you'd say, "Oh, hello, hello. How're you getting on? Good to see you." And you used to see them sometimes turn up with a new babe. Perhaps teenagers would come down with their parents one year, and you come down the next year and they're married and got a babe. It was absolutely exciting. I was the only daughter in my family, but my father's brother had three daughters and they'd all got lovely long red hair, like mine. And when we used to go there, 'Oh, hello Nelly, how are you? You've grown." "I'm not Nelly, I'm Marjorie." "Which one's Mary? Which one's Cathy?" And we were that much alike. But when we got down there we could hear the people say, "Cor, there's those Worrows again; they're taking over the blooming place!" there were so many of us.

Marjorie Balcombe

We might arrive at Tonbridge about four o'clock in the morning, get outside the station, on a side street it was – didn't go the main front way – and it'd be pitch black, all cold and misty, dewy. And we had to wait there until the wagon came to pick us up. Some farmers used to come there about nine o'clock, ten o'clock. Most of them come in the afternoon to pick them up. We'd left home, Spitalfield, at eleven o'clock the previous night. On the train all night, got off four o'clock, sat outside. Some of the men and women, the fitter ones, they used to leave us with the luggage, they'd walk down the farm about six or seven mile, and get the best hut they could have, and make up the bed. The farmer used to chuck two bales of straw in, about four faggots.

Mike Fitzgerald

I married into a hop-picking family. They'd all been going years before me. I didn't start till I was about twenty, but I soon got used to it. When I saw the huts, I nearly dropped. You had loads of straw and you had to make a bed up, so if you didn't take a mattress cover with you, you were stuck. My mother-in-law had told me to take a mattress cover with me and she saw me all right.

The farmer used to deliver what they called faggots, tree twigs and branches, about a yard long, all done up in a big bundle. They used to give you so many bundles for a hut. Of course you lived rent free as well. You made the beds up while the men lit the fires up outside. My husband used to do ours, for his mother and me.

The first day you'd get yourselves all comfortable, as comfortable as you could, and you sort of adjusted to it as you went along. I had my husband with me and he was used to it, so he knew what he was doing. He made an underground oven, dug it out of the ground, got a big round tin, put it in the hole, and then built the fire round it, so you could cook on it.

There was my husband, me and the baby – he was ten months old.

First day of work, I went to the farmhouse to get a hot loaf, a lump of cheese or corned beef – it was cheap then, you know – and brought it back and buttered it, and cut it up, ready for twelve o'clock when they blew the whistle for lunch. And silly me, being so green, I put it at the back of the baby's push chair. Course, when they blew the whistle for lunch, we've got no food. He'd eaten it. Ten months old. I'm not kidding, believe me, I'm not kidding. He'd eaten the whole loaf. Weren't he good? While I was picking hops, he was doing that. He was sitting in the pushchair all morning, at the side of us, you know. Course we never had a chance to look at him because we were working. Anyway, he was behaving himself so much, we didn't bother. Course when we looked round, we got nothing for dinner. He'd finished it up, he'd eaten the loaf, the corned beef, everything.

Anyway, the next morning, my mother-in-law says to me, "Give me that bag here." She says, "He's not eating that today." So she took my food and kept it with theirs. Course, the baby's looking round all the morning for food. It was funny.

Ellen Russell

If you went every year, you used to label your things, pack them into the tin bath, cover them and store them in a big room over by the oast house. My gran used to put lino down on the floor of her hut, so at the end of the season she would put her broom in it tie it all up with a label on. The first day there, they used to open up the oast, and call your name and fetch your things out, and you would go over and collect the things you left there.

Joan Clarkson

A crowded hut (photo lent by Charlotte Fowler)

We used to pick on Lily Farm. Claudie, the farmer there, was lovely. He knew everybody by their names. It was quite a small farm compared to other farms. There were about twenty huts. We liked working on the same farm where everybody knew each other. It felt like a big family. Almost everyone there was a relation of ours in some way or other.

Anne Fitzgerald

We'd bring an old tea chest to pack all the junk in. That would be turned upside down outside the hut, with American cloth over it. American cloth was like baize; you could wipe it or you could wash it. It had white baize at the back and it was patterned – green or red – it was fairly thick. So you would have that on the tables, like a table cloth.

Laura Murphy

People literally used to pack up their home into a big quilt and take it. For stools, we'd have apple boxes to sit on. You all slept together in this one great big bed. They painted the walls inside of the huts, and made them as homely as they could. You had apple boxes for your furniture, but it was just all really primitive.

Flo Batley

21

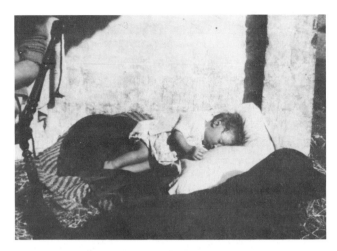

Baby Kathleen settles into the hop hut
(photo lent by Kathleen Ash)

They used to give us bundles of brushwood done up in a bundle for our fires and for under the bed. The first thing I did was to mark out the space for the fire in the dirt and dig it out. Then you take out the metal of your oven that you brought with you from London. And you broke up the smallest twigs all from your faggots, put them on a piece of paper, lit the paper and the wood started going. Then you'd go and fill up your big pots with water. And you'd put that water on there to boiling point, and you made your big pot of tea, for how many there was, four or five. You made your tea.

Well I used to be head cook and bottle-washer, so it was always my job to make tea when we got there. And while I'm doing that, the kids have started pulling the straw to pieces and they're filling their pillowcases up. Well then after we've all had a cup of tea and perhaps a sandwich we'd brought down with us, we start filling up the mattress. Then you fill up the other mattress for the children. You'd sweep your hut out and then you lay these mattresses on the papers or sheets, whatever you want, and then you put your sheets on and your blankets.

Then you go out and you have a walk round to see where you are and what you're up to. Then you've got whatever you brought down with you for lunch that day, and the kids go round and play whatever they want until it starts to get dusk. Then they all draw in front of the huts, and start making friends with one another. We had quite a few friends down there, and the kids made their own friends. They used to find some water to go down the dykes catching tiddlers.

Ethel Neighbour

A HANDY LARDER

They used to get a big seven pound biscuit tin and put all the margarine, butter, bacon, cheese and stuff like that in it. Then they'd dig a hole in the ground, round about the same size; then put something inside so it went down the edges, and put water in the hole. Then they'd put the tin lid on tight, and then bury it. And that was a little larder. It was wonderful.

Harry Demarne

I didn't like it when I first stayed in the hop hut. All that straw! I went to bed with my hat and coat on and my wellington boots. I didn't want spiders or anything running round me! The next day, I went to the village and got myself some digs for the rest of the week. I only stayed the one week.

Dot Seadon

One year, we went hop-picking at Staplehurst. We went into this hut, you know, and made it all nice. But, during the night, my Mum was crying. The woman in the next hut was a friend of hers and she shouted through "What's the matter?" My Mum said, "There's mice running up and down the curtains!" She was terrified of mice.

Ruby Jones

But they were the real poor times, weren't they. My mum said that when she first went she was a young wife, and she was very particular, she still is. And it was murder for her down there, she was too particular. All my Dad's family said, "You're too fussy." But she soon got used to it. She loved it.

Anne Fitzgerald

My brother Michael by our hut (photo lent by Nell Mason)

THE HOP HUTS

Marjorie Balcombe's family outside their hut.

When we got to the farm, we were given wooden huts, the huts that they used to store all their stuff in through the winter. And I suppose the hut itself was about fourteen foot square. A third of it was living area and the rest was a white-washed wooden slatted bed like a big bench coming out from the wall. It had a chalk floor, hard trodden down chalk on earth, no wooden floors or anything like that. We took our own rugs that we made, either knitted or made with hooks that you pull the wool through, to cover the floor area. The black box, my grandma's tin trunk, sat there like a bedside table. We didn't empty it out because we had no cupboards, no nothing. We'd take a bit of wall paper and a bit of net curtain to pin to the door.

The bed itself was made out of faggots, they were twigs from the trees tied in bundles. And they were brought round and delivered at your door. And you picked these faggots up and you took them inside the hut, you cut the cord, and you laid these faggots out. And then we had a mattress cover, and they gave us straw. So we filled this mattress cover full up with straw, put that on top of the faggots, and that was our bed. I used to sleep with my parents. Sometimes there was a gap in the middle of the bed and then a separate bit of bed. My two brothers used to sleep in that other little bit. But you could go back the next year and they'd fill that piece in, so it was one great big long bed. So when it was like that, all the ladies slept up one end, and all the men up the other end, and all their feet met in the midle. Because when my father came down, perhaps

he'd fetch his friends with him. So there was all the men one end and all the ladies the other.

You'd see families of ten and twelve in the huts. And we took our dog with us, our Queeny. We had our own blankets, no sheets, and our own pillow cases stuffed with straw. And there were galvanised roofs. So if it poured with rain, you never got no sleep. Rattled! It used to go like mad. Then for our lighting we had hurricane lamps, the old fashioned hurricane lamps with paraffin in the wick. Or candles. Perhaps if you were lucky enough or could afford it, you had a primus stove.

Marjorie Balcombe

If you went from your hut to the next hut or the next hut, you'd see all the old women there, wearing their black caps. All the mothers had clean pinafores on in the evenings. They'd do their washing outside the hut. They would put a big bucket on the fire, and they'd put their washing in that. Behind the huts, they had clothes lines to put all their washing on. They used to fit in all the chores, even though they'd been picking all day. They'd do the washing in the evening or get up early and boil up the clothes. They had just one tap in the middle of the common, a communal one. Take the clothes and rinse them under the tap and then wring them out and hang them up.

Eileen O'Sullivan

When you got to the farm, there's some huts. And when I say they are huts, they're sheds, really. They'd been open all the year round. Well, you might have five or six or even eight people in one hut – all sharing the same bed. The women would be up one end of the bed and the men and boys down the other. If one turned over, you all turned! They were tin huts and very cold inside. The next morning, you'd be awake at five o'clock because somebody up there would be talking. The hut itself would be about eight foot wide, so you could hear your neighbours easily.

Stanley Rose

The first hut I had of my own at Whitbread's was one of the ordinary corrugated iron shed huts with a platform for a bed. But after a while I got one of these wooden huts with an upstairs. Some of the Whitbread huts were wooden and some of the older ones were corrugated iron. They had an upstairs ... like a ladder, going up to an upstairs with a platform downstairs where you put your bed. You didn't actually sleep on the floor although they did years and years and years ago. At first we used to take the big mattress covers and they would provide you with straw to fill them. You did the same upstairs, so you had a big bed upstairs that went the whole width of the hut. As the years went on and you travelled down by lorry, you would load it up with your own mattress from home. Also lots of people had calor gas stoves, but we didn't, we still used to cook in the cookhouse.

You'd make sure you always had a lot of dry wood, overnight you'd heap it up inside your hut and then you'd to be up early in the morning, get a faggot of wood and paper and light it up – whoosh! The pot would boil and you'd make the tea, and you had enough hot water to wash the kids, without going up to fetch it. But, at Whitbread's, you could walk up to a tent and get your hot water all the time. Take the bucket and get it full of hot water and come back and wash the kids.

Kathleen Ash

We took a photo of our old hop hut. If you look at it now, you'd never believe that human beings used to live in there for six weeks! We only had the one bed. We used to have all the kids in the bed, have the kids there in the middle of the bed, with my mum at one extreme end, then the kids, and I'd go on the other end. When my husband came down for the weekend, of course we all had to sleep in the same bed, so my mum used to have a curtain as a partition in the bed between us and the rest of the family. One time, he got out in the middle of the night to do a wee, and when he got back into bed, he got in the wrong side with my mum! He put his arm round her, just to snuggle up, and my mum's saying, "Minnie! Come and take him away, he don't know where he is!" and I'm saying, "Come over here, come over here. You're in the wrong side of the bed!"

Minnie Martin

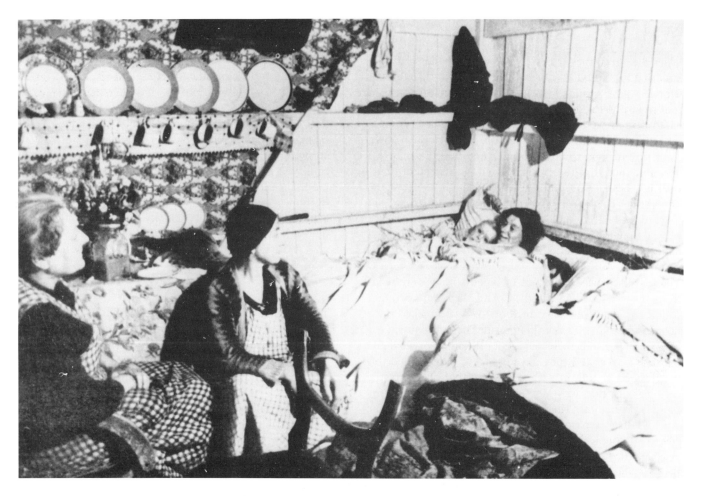

Snug in bed in a hop hut (photo lent by Whitbread Hop Farm)

Outside the hut 1932 (photo lent by Charlotte Fowler)

We used to take up a row of huts with our two families! The huts were made of corrugated iron and were about ten foot by twelve. Some families had eight or nine kids in there. If you had that many, you'd get a double hut – if you were lucky! You used to take the panel off in between two huts and make a door so you didn't have to go outside. We used to wait until everybody had arrived who had booked to come in, and if someone hadn't arrived, you could have their hut. We used to wallpaper the huts ... and have orange boxes up-ended with a curtain on the front for a food cabinet. When we first started going as kids, we'd put bales of wood that they called faggots on the floor, put the straw on top, and that was our bed. But then later on, we started taking our own beds. They started putting electricity in the huts as well.

Bet Easterbrook

We used to have two huts. We used one for cooking in and one for sleeping in ... five or six would sleep in a hut. Then you used to have your bowls and all that outside the hut so you could do all the washing up ... we were properly organised!

Charlotte Fowler

When you arrived at the huts, the first thing you did, you used to have a tick, you know, on the mattress covers. You'd undo that, get the straw and you'd fill that up, all the kids would be filling it up, you'd hold it. And then my mum would sow it up. And you'd start your bed on the floor.

Faggots, brushwood bundle. But as the years progressed it got a bit more comfortable, and my mum would say all year round, "Oh that'll do for hopping. Don't throw anything out. Nice table." Then she put all curtains round the bed. The hut was minute. So you'd have this much room to live. That was the bed there, and at the end of your bed you'd have a little table, table outside.

Our old hut we had was corrugated iron, and there was a gap where the sides didn't reach the ceiling so everybody could hear every word you said. You could hear everything. "You alright? What you up to in there?" and all that.

There was a hole in one. "Don't you look through this hole," she said, "I'm having a wash." "Put a bit of paper over it then." Mum used to make a hole purposely, to have a little picture. I'd be climbing up, looking, knowing me.

You'd hear people shout at the kids sometimes. Some of them were a bit rough, weren't they? But not really.

Anne Fitzgerald

You done all your cooking outside. Any washing up, you had a table outside, with a bowl on it to put your water in and wash your gear. If it was raining, all the kids had to go to bed – an early night!

Tom Easterbrook

There might be another forty families working on the same farm. The first row of huts were mostly taken by our family. Then there was another row of huts and they were lived in by people from Bermondsey. Then over the other side there was a little common and a big family over there from Stepney. This was a particularly large hop farm. The same huts were there year after year. In the winter, animals were put in them, but they were well cleaned out ready for the hop-pickers and done up with some lime stuff every year, so they weren't smelly. There were a lot of creepy-crawleys so my mum used to take sprays and things.

The actual hop huts were all white distemper and it used to be horrible, so my mum used to buy all the odd rolls of wall paper – it didn't matter what pattern – and a bag of flour (any flour) and we could mix it up like dough, put it on the wallpaper and it used to stick on the walls and hide the distemper and it looked much better. We took the lino off the floors back home to put on the floor of the hut and afterwards took it back home again. It wasn't uncommon – the majority of pickers did the same.

The huts weren't heated, but they weren't cold. If it was cold we couldn't take a paraffin stove down because my mum couldn't afford one. In later years, some people took Calor gas cookers along and they had dinner in their hop hut. The beds used to come half way along the hut and in the other half you would eat the food and so on. If it was weather, we'd have a table outside. We didn't have to the tables and chairs down on the train: this is where le were good to us down there because if they had

tables and chairs, they used to give them to my mum and then we'd leave them in the hop hut and lock it up each year and the farmer used to keep the key. The first time you went and you knew you were going to that farm every year you used to just leave things there and only bring your bed linen home.

Where I went you had to keep your hut clean as well as all the surroundings. People who say that hop-picking is dirty must have gone to a dirty farm. If people came down who weren't clean, the farmer would use his own judgement if he thought they were going to be trouble makers. He would give them a chance, but some weren't picking, just using the hut as a holiday place. Some people did. One year we decided to go to Hunton hop-picking, just for a change. We didn't like that farm: it wasn't very clean. My younger brother, John, was six at the time. He used to go missing at the same time every day, so my mum had him followed. He used to go to the workhouse in Workhouse Lane and bring food home with him because he told the people that we were very poor.

When I first went hop-picking I was six months old. This was in 1919. One of my brothers was practically born down there. As a baby I used to go out into the field with my mum, in a pram. The pram we took our luggage in was also used as a bed to keep the babies in to save putting them in the straw. When I got married I used to take my own bed and wardrobes and things like that. Some people used to take pianos and gas cookers!

Kit O'Connell

Tea for two (photo lent by Whitbread Hop Farm)

My gran picked for Whitbread, until the year she died, and then my mother took her ticket over. Whitbread's was always a model farm. Most hop farms they had just one-storey huts. You had one room, where you ate and slept. At Whitbread's, there were two-storey huts – quite flash really. They were brick built at the bottom, but the upstairs was built of tin. You had a tin roof with a skylight, which was lovely when you could see the sun, and the stars and things, but people used to paint them to keep out the light. When it used to rain it used to bang on the tin roof!

They're still there, the huts, to the best of my knowledge. Across from us there was a row of one-storey single wooden huts. My gran was always afraid of fire, so she would never have had one of those.

Joan Clarkson

The huts used to look really homely in the end because you got to the stage where you had the same huts every year – we used to go down August Bank Holiday and we used to call it white-wash day, go down and white-wash all the huts, ready for when we went in September.

You only had one big bed in there. We had two huts, but there could be as many as six or seven in each hut. I'd have to sleep with my nan and my mum and my cousins who might come. And there might be three people in a single bed; there might be four or five of us women in a big bed, which was all lumpy. When the men came, they all got in another bed together. When we had all these extra people like cousins, and the menfolk and friends, which invariably did happen, they all came, you just had to make do.

1953 The Bowers' family at their hop hut

We all used to talk to each other across the top of the huts, because you could actually stand on the table and look over and see them all in bed in the next hut. So privacy wasn't even in it. When the parents were out, the kids used to lark about and throw things over and talk.

Elaine Jones

Charlotte Fowler and her family outside their hop hut, 1932

THE WORKING DAY

AN EARLY START

The stickie was the knocker-up ... he had a stick and he'd come and bang on the doors of the huts in the morning to get us all up ... we all used to shout at him to go away!

Tom Easterbrook

About seven, the farmer'd come along, old Claude, with his basket, and he'd get near the huts, the corrugated iron huts where we were, and pick up a brick, and bang on the side, bang! Old Claude's here! "Come on, all to work!" The pole pullers used to get up and follow him along. I used to creep up about half an hour later! We had thirty bins; we were all one family.

Mike Fitzgerald

When you went up to the fields, it was always a cold morning; foggy and damp. And yet you pulled that bine. And then in the afternoon it would be boiling hot. And your hands would get dirty and black and smelly. Hop hands. And then you didn't have any bath or anything. You used to fill the bowl up and have a wash down. And there'd be about – how many people in the bed? About six or twelve.

Anne Fitzgerald

We was all up early in the morning, all wash in cold water, all used the same water. The children had to go and get the water in a galvanised bucket. We used to have a long pole, which we'd hold at each end, put the pole through the buckets and go and get everybody's water. We'd say "Do you want any water Mrs Smith, Mrs White, Mrs Jones?" Four or five children used to take it in turns. Or, other than that, used to take a saucepan. And if you wanted a drink you used to take this saucepan with the lid and used to drink out of the lid at the tap.

Marjorie Balcombe

Every morning, I'd get up first and go and get a couple of buckets of water from the tap up the field. If there wasn't a tap, a tank would come along on a horse-drawn wagon. Then I'd get a fire going in the cookhouse. This was a very large, open-ended Anderson shelter, with several hearths all the way through. I used to fill the hopping pot with water, then get a piece of rag, place a handful of tea leaves, a pile of sugar and a tin of condensed milk in it, tie it up and put it in the boiling water. To avoid a smoky taste I used to put in a couple of twigs and this would absorb the smoke. I think we used to have bread and jam for breakfast.

Tom Baldwin

Arriving at the fields (photo lent by Whitbread Hop Farm)

As a little girl going hop-picking I would have to get up at six o'clock in the morning and light the fire, getting water from a tap quite close to the huts. A faggot man used to come round with the faggots for the fire. So we used to get the water boiling. Breakfast would be porridge or toast and tea out of the pot, in enamel mugs. We didn't have posh cups and saucers.

Then the bailiff would come down. He was actually a foreman but we used to call him the bailiff. He would come around, call out your name and tell you which hop set you were going into and the number of your bin – all the bins had numbers. There used to be a chap with a van who came round early in the morning with hot bread. Then you would go up to the hop field with your kettle and your pot, and my mum would make up all sorts of sandwiches. She'd take a loaf of bread up there and cut it up with onions and cheese and whatever.

I used to hate the early mornings when you pulled in the bins of hops. The bines used to be covered in dew and you got soaking wet. All the children had to help or else when the lolly man came round you never got a lolly. He used to sell all sorts of sweets, but we always called him the lolly man.

Kit O'Connell

You'd get up in the morning, and there'd be a mist everywhere. You'd have to have a cold wash outside the hut, then you'd have to carry the chairs and the sandwiches up to the field. You had to carry all that, and sometimes it was quite a long walk, because you weren't always near the hop fields, and you were carrying chairs and boxes to sit on, the coats and flasks and the food. We used to plead that my mum made the sandwiches and not my nan, because if my nan did them, they tasted of paraffin. It was all paraffin oil lamps and she always managed to get paraffin over all the sandwiches, everything. We used to get down there and think, "Ugh!" because they all tasted of paraffin.

You'd get down to the bins and pull the bines, and they'd all be covered in dew, so you'd get soaked. You had to go out in the morning really wrapped up, because September's getting quite cold, and by about ten o'clock everybody's shedding clothes.

Elaine Jones

We used to go out to the hop fields about seven o'clock in the morning where the bines were climbing up on wires; as you pulled them down all the dew come down ... you'd get a shower! And your hands would all be black from the hops. The stain had a bitter taste, ever so bitter. And the old farmer used to say, "Go on, you don't want paper round your bread; it's good for you, a tonic!" If you didn't wear a hat or scarf or something on your head, you'd get all sulphur in your hair – that could make your head come up in bumps.

Vi Lewis

In the morning, you'd have a cup of tea, take some in the flask, and away you go to the hop fields. You got on all the oldest clothes you could think of wearing. You get in your line, or row, and you have to pull these bines down. Now they're heavy with dew, absolutely pouring with dew, and you had to pull them, because you've got to pluck them, take the hops off them. Of course you get soaked. So you pull the bines down, then you start to break the hops off. They were like little acorns, but they was much softer. And there's loads of them on this bine, and then you have to keep moving it around until you've cleaned the lot off. And then that bine you hang over the wires, and then away you go to the next bine. Now and again, naturally, you'd have a chat, and sometimes you'd have a little sing-song, sometimes you would take over the whole garden, and sing the old numbers, the very old numbers, "Me and my girl." – anything that was going in them days. It wasn't all hardship, it was happiness as well, because it was so unusual to home. So, you're doing that picking. You stop to make your cup of tea; again you make your little fire and cook something there. And then away you go, back to stripping the bines – you keep going. And then, every so often, the man comes round and takes all you've picked, empties out the bin, puts the tally on a card, which he gives back to you, and then there's so much earned on that card, which you can now borrow at the end of the week from the farmer.

Stanley Rose

Dot Seadon and her younger sister picking on the bins

The Fitzgerald family make an early start

ON THE FIELDS

If it was cold in the morning, we always wore gloves. Wouldn't take them off to pick hops. I only remember being rained off once or twice. If it was raining very badly, you had to go back to the huts, because you couldn't pick in the heavy rain.

You know what September mornings are like, dewy and misty, and I didn't like it in the morning, it was cold. When you pulled the bine down, you got showered, didn't you, with all the dew and the water, and everything. I didn't like that, because you would feel wet. My gran and my mother used to laugh it off. But that's the sort of thing I remember. You used to pull the bine down, throw it over the bin, and then start pulling off the branches and picking. When the bines are picked, you wind them up and leave them until the whole field is cleared. You see, you used to have to leave everything tidy behind you.

When you'd picked all the bines each side of your bin, you would pick your bin up and you would move it along the row. As children, you'd be sent back to pick up any hops that fell on the floor. Sort of like gleaning corn, because you weren't allowed to leave them on the floor.

Joan Clarkson

Two or three people would go and look at the crop and see what the hops were like. They would negotiate the charge for picking the hops. If they were very large ones they'd have to do five bushels for a shilling; if they were small ones, they'd do four, or three bushels for a shilling because they were hard work.

The measurer used to come round and they used to sing a song about the measurer:

> They are lovely hops
> They are lovely hops
> When the measurer he comes round
> Pick 'em up, pick 'em up off the ground.
>
> When he starts to measure 'em
> He doesn't know when to stop
> Aye, aye, that's your lot
> Push in the bloody lot.

Of course the people used to get the hops and lift them up so they were loose, then the measurer used to come along and force them in to the baskets, squash them down.

You got five or six kids round the bin, picking all day, from half past seven in the morning to five at night. They would do very well. They'd save a few bob out of it. After a day or two, they used to ask for a sub, and the manager of the farm would give them that.

Harry Demarne

You had to get up early to be at the fields. The bins were heavy to carry. My mother used to get the men to carry our bin from field to field. They'd throw me in the bin and they'd carry me along. After they'd finished picking the bines in one place, they'd move along, and my job was to go along the line with me hat, picking up all the hops that had fallen. Really fun. We used to go to Lamberhurst in Kent. The farmer was very nice. His name was Mr Day, and that was when the song came out, "Happy days are here again." Well when we saw the farmer coming, those up the top end used to start singing, "Happy days are here again." And everybody started singing so that they would give all the others a warning that Mr Day was coming round. I used to love picking. The only thing I didn't like was lunch-time. At midday, we always had cheese and bread and when you picked your bread up, it was all hoppy – ooh, horrible it used to be. So bitter! The bread was always yellow where you kept handling it.

Ruby Jones

Pullling the bines down, you got ladybirds, you got caterpillars, you got spiders. To catch a caterpillar and put it in a matchbox was great. Something you didn't see in London.

Lilian Carter

My dad was a pole puller. The bines grow in fours, and as you pull them down over the bin you sometimes leave the head behind. My dad's job was to go along the rows with his pole with a hook on the end and knock down all the heads because they were the best of the hops.

Florence Burgess

It was a bit hard getting going in the mornings down there. You'd get out of bed, get dressed and open the door to let the air in. You couldn't just go downstairs and turn the tap on, you had to walk a certain way to get your water. If you were sensible, you filled up your bucket the night before, but then you still had to walk away to spend a penny. The toilets were miles away.

Then you put your pot on for your tea. When that's done and you're drinking the tea, there'd be embers died down at the fire, and when they're still hot, you put your six or seven slices of bread for the kids on the griddle to toast it. While they're eating that, you'd go down and fill the pot up, you'd come back and put the pot back on the fire, you'd build that fire up, and clear up a bit. You leave the bed open to let it air. And then the kids all had to take it in turns with a drop of hot water out of that second pot and all have a wash, and tie our hair up in a scarf before we went up the top. So it was always nice and clean. The old ladies used to put plenty of clothes on and a nice clean apron to go up there.

Ethel Neighbour

Everyday, before you went on the hop fields, the straw had to be shaken up, because by morning, it would be all flat. So you used to have to shake the straw, shake the pillows, make the bed and tidy up. And then wipe down the table outside, take everything in, and then pack all the sandwiches. You'd take a kettle of water with you, for the field ... and always a tin teapot, with tea and sugar already in it. And then you went up the field. Nobody was allowed in the huts during the day ... because you were taken down to do a job.

Laura Murphy

Florence Burgess's parents in the hop field

"All in the one field" (photo lent by John Wardley)

When you got the bine, you laid it over the bin, and first you took the leaves off and left them on the floor, and then you had to be careful, because if you got a scratch from a bine, you knew you had it; you got a great big scar. The bines were rough, very rough. Like a very rough rope. They could cut you across your arm. You didn't pick the hops off separately, you'd be there for evermore. You picked the leaves off and then you scoured through. That's when you could get like a rope burn from the bine. You could tie up anything with a bine. They were very, very tough. A lot of us used to have an old stocking pulled up on to the top of our arms. Some wore old gloves and all. Oh, it was shocking if you got a burn! When they pulled the bines down, sometimes one would fall across your arm, so you got that mark right up your arm.

Peg King

You didn't have a choice about the row you worked on. When your row was finished, the farmer or whoever was in charge of the field would put you on the next vacant one. You'd pick up your bin, and you'd walk right along to the next row. You only had to look at the row to know if you'd got a good row of bines or not. Some are very sparse and others are loaded. You couldn't move up to a loaded one. Sometimes you'd have a moan. You'd say, "We're not

going to get much out of this," and the quicker you picked that row and get on to the next one the better.

It could be a bit competitive. You were chasing the pickers in front. And you'd pick your bin up and you'd go to your next four bines and you'd look around and say, more or less, "Oh, they've moved a bit sharpish. Come on, pick, get going!" because it's chasing money. That's what you were doing at the end of it. I presume that's why – we never had holidays – my dad took up hop-picking. Because there was money involved.

Lilian Carter

The family was never split up and sent to different fields. We were all in the one field until we had picked it. There would probably be my mother, my eldest sister and two older brothers on the bin. In the front of the furrow of hops we younger children each had a bucket or a basket and we had to fill up so many hops before we got our sweets. If you felt tired or ill you were allowed to lie down. That was okay as long as you weren't pretending.

We did have a proper lunch break when the bailiff blew his whistle. We used to have an hour's break. Sometimes the kids were allowed to go off and have a play, but mostly they were picking.

Kit O'Connell

32

DIRTY WORK

The hops stained clothes. A brown stain. Your fingers are brown when you've finished hop-picking and you have to get it off with soda and stuff – all sorts of things we had to use. It was very hard to get off. Grandma used to put soda and hot water in the bowl and we used to scrub until it came off, you know, and it'd wear off in time. But the hop-pickers' hands were brown at the end of the season – apart from being brown with the sun, because the weather always seemed to be warm in those days except for the sharp showers.

If you were there for six weeks hop-picking – people who came down from London – you didn't have a lot of washing water (there were no taps laid on in the huts they lived in). I suppose when they got home it wore off working and doing the washing. Don't forget, everybody did their washing by hand in those days, so the mothers would easily get rid of the stain on wash day, with soda in the water and that soap that had soda in it.

Joan Miller

You never went and washed your hands during the day, because you were right out in the fields. You got this green on your fingers and it had a sort of acid taste. Then the cake man would come along with the cakes on a little tray, and you'd sit there with a cheese cake, or one of the ones with a cherry on top, you'd eat one of these. Or there was one like a cone with coconut on top – they used to get Tottenham cake which was an ordinary sponge with icing on top. The old ice cream tricycle, the Stop Me And Buy One, used to come round too! They brought it to the entrance of the hop-field. They used to have what we now call ice lollies – in a sort of a triangle ... Wall's made them. Also a van came round with the fish and chips ... the bell would go, and we'd all make a beeline for it!

Bob Bennett

Mum used to make us coarse aprons. A thin sack with strings on the end to tie round us. We all had our big aprons round us. So when we picked, we had the bines lying across the apron. But you were dirty all the same. The alley ways where you walked would be thick with mud.

We had poles for the hop bines, that's why they always called the person who'd pull the poles up a pole puller. He'd pull the poles up, and take the bine to the bin. But when we had string, the pole puller used to lift the bin along the drift for you, and you pulled your own string. But after you'd pulled down them four strings and you'd finished picking the hops off, you had to roll up the bines so it looked like a little ball. On other farms, you'd just have thrown the empty bines on the ground: but our boss was fussy, he liked his hop garden tidy. When all hop picking was finished, all you could see was a row of hop balls where all the bines were wound up. My husband and the other men used to cut them off with a hook and the women used to pick them up and put them in the horse and cart and they used to be burnt. Then the field was ploughed and everything, ready for next year. The roots of the hops were still there you see, what they call the heel. Then the men used to cut them in January to the beginning of February and we'd start all over again.

Alice Heskitt

Mike Fitzgerald (pole puller) and some relatives at the bin

WORK IN THE HOP FIELDS

September 1931

Hops are trained up poles or over wires about ten feet high, and grown in rows a yard or two apart. All the pickers have to do is to tear them down and strip the hops into a bin, keeping them as clean as possible of leaves. In practice, of course, it is impossible to keep all the leaves out, and the experienced pickers swell the bulk of their hops by putting in just as many leaves as the farmer will stand for. One soon gets the knack of the work, and the only hardships are the standing (we were generally on our feet ten hours a day), the plagues of plant lice, and the damage to one's hands. One's hands get stained as black as a Negro's with the hop-juice, which only mud will remove, and after a day or two they crack and are cut to bits by the stems of the vines, which are spiny. In the mornings, before the cuts had reopened, my hands used to give me perfect agony, and even at the time of typing this (10 October) they show the marks. Most of the people who go down hopping have done it every year since they were children, and they pick like lightning and know all the tricks, such as shaking the hops up to make them lie loose in the bin, etc. The most successful pickers are families, who have two or three adults to strip the vines, and a couple of children to pick up the fallen hops and clear the odd strands. The laws about child labour are disregarded utterly, and some of the people drive their children pretty hard. The woman in the next bin to us, a regular old-fashioned East Ender, kept her grandchildren at it like slaves – "Go on, Rose, you lazy little cat, pick them 'ops up. I'll warm your arse if I get up to you," etc., until the children, aged from six to ten, used to drop down and fall asleep on the ground. But they liked the work, and I don't supppose it did them more harm than school

George Orwell, Collected Essays

*The Withers family in hop fields
(photo lent by Elaine Johns)*

The quicker you picked the hops the better it was; so the more people taken down there, the more they were expected to pick. The hops have to be picked at a certain time. If you don't pick them and the rain gets to them, the hops go all soggy, and then they're not much good. They've got to be picked when they're ready, and as quick as possible – like fruit really. The pole pullers used to come along and undo the bines from the top. It was all on the strings, and they would loosen that bine from the top of the string, and then you would pull it down yourself; you would have the bine over your knees most of the time and you'd pick into the bin. Or if you had children, the younger ones would sit near a basket, you'd break a piece of the bine off and give it to them and the children would pick that into the basket. So we all had to work. People would sing. Somebody would start singing, and everybody else would join in. All the old fashioned songs; all the very old songs. We used to mostly sing all day and the kids would be bawling and shouting. But it was good, very good. And all the old mums, you could hear the mums chatting across the field to one another. Before you got into the hop fields, you'd have all the bines, so you couldn't see the people, and it wasn't until you pulled them all down that you could see who was on the next row.

I remember everybody stopping for lunch. They used to blow a whistle, and we'd stop for half an hour. We couldn't wash our hands. I don't know if you've ever tasted anything that's "hoppy"? Ooh, it's bitter. Bitter! But we used to have to eat our food with it. We'd make a little fire up the back of the field, not near the hops, and make the tea and eat our sandwiches. Then the whistle would go, and we had to get back to work.

So we all lived in the huts and we all went to the fields together. But most of the men who worked in the fields were locals. They would come round measuring the hops as we turned them into the bins. They were strict in the way that, if you had leaves in your bin, you used to have to pick them out: you weren't allowed to put in what they called "dirty hops" – they'd refuse to take them. They'd come round and measure up the hops in your bin. Well they would shake them, and the hops would go down further, and they would say it wasn't a full bin. You'd think you had filled two bins, you'd only have one and half there! So they wouldn't give you the amount of money you should have had for that ... "Ooh, them again – shaking the hops!" It wasn't fair to us, because we'd been picking them all day, and they'd come and shake them to make the hops sink down lower. The lorry would come round, about twice in the morning, twice in the afternoon. The men would come down and measure the hops, and take them away to the oast house.

Laura Murphy

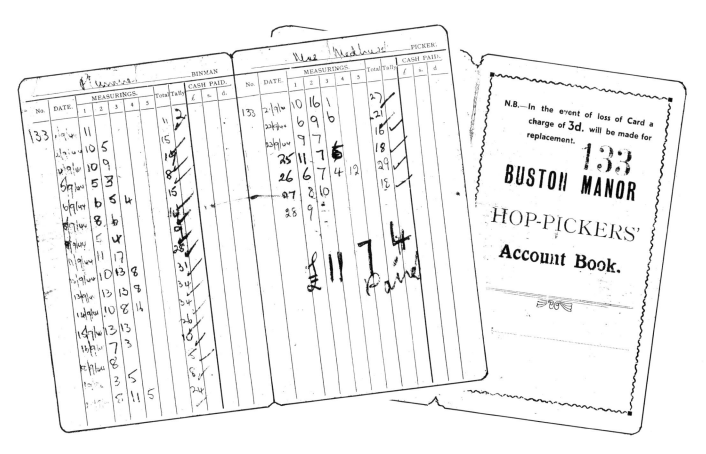

Hop-pickers account book (lent by Mr. Medhurst)

THE MEASURER

There was a bit of competitiveness about it, how many bushels the woman in the next bin had picked, you've got to beat her today because she's done, you know, so many.

Then they'd all be saying, "Oh, your bins are dirty." A dirty bin meant you left leaves in it. People used to say that the ones who were getting lots of bushels were leaving their bins dirty. When they called, "Pull no more bines," it meant the measurer was going to come and measure up for you, and you had to clean your bin out fast. You should've seen my grandmother and mother clean their bin; they used to get all the leaves out quickly. People actually took a pride in cleaning their bins, getting all the leaves out. But what it actually meant was that you wouldn't earn as much because it was lighter. Usually you did clean as you went along, you would scoop them up and clean them every now and again, but then when he said, "Pull no more bines," and he was coming round to measure, you had to stop picking.

There was a great discipline to hop-picking; you didn't start until he blew the whistle. And as soon as he blew the whistle again, you stopped. You had to just sit there and watch until he'd gone along and measured everybody's bins, which he did a couple of times a day. They'd watch him and say, "Oh, you're taking them heavy." It meant he was filling his basket up too much. I think a lot of people would buy him drinks in the pub and he would take their measure light.

Elaine Jones

My gran picked because she was a widow and she needed the money. She had children to support, and her kids had to pick too. My grandmother's been told off by the measurer. She picked too many leaves. If there were too many leaves, they didn't withhold payment, but they would tell you to clean them up. If they were what they called dirty – too many leaves – they wouldn't even measure them. They'd say, "Clean your hops." But you see, if she could get away with it she would.

If I wanted to pick, she used to get a piece of string and put it round the end of the bin and tie up about a quarter of the bin. She used to get me to pick into that, because I only picked hops – I didn't pick leaves! And then when the measurer was coming round, she used to untie mine and throw them on top to make it look better, and shuffle all hers underneath. I used to have to pick the leaves out of my gran's because my mum had her own bin, you see, and she picked very clean.

The measurer would come round with a bushel or a two bushel basket. I know you used to be paid so much for two bushels. It wasn't a lot of money, and most people used to sub their money every few days, so what they earned they used to go and sub it. And at the end of hop-picking they didn't have a lot of money. Some people did quite well. A whole family would go and they really would pick. What my grandmother used to call them! Because she thought they were greedy, you see. I mean her language could be very ripe.

Joan Clarkson

Measuring the hops (photo lent by Eileen O'Sullivan)

Some of the men used to bring a pint of the beer from the pub and take it up the field and they would sit there in the lovely sunshine and a nice bit of bread and cheese and a drop of beer or a cup of tea or whatever it was. We'd break for our lunches for about an hour. If you wanted to get back picking sooner, you did. Sometimes they'd call out, "Lunchtime." or "Dinner." "Knock off for dinner." Then at night they'd call out, "Pull no more bines!" And that meant, "That's it, you've had it." So if you had a watch, you'd think, "Four o'clock. They'll be calling out soon." You didn't pull a bine down and leave it overnight, because it would go a bit soft. And while they're firm they come off more easily. There were four bines in a heel – and you worked, you worked, you worked; then every now and again you went back, and you got those bines together, and you coiled them round, tied them, so you left them tidy. The overseer would come round with a stick, have a look to see if you've left all the tails on – because the heads were the thickest part; the tails were single bits that came out, they would be more fiddly. But the heads would be thick, plenty of hops on, and you'd get going on them. So the overseer would lift up the bine and make sure you never left all the tails. You were supposed to clear your ground up. Obviously, when you pulled the bine down, some fell off. And you would pick them up. If the overseer saw you'd left any hops behind on the ground, he'd make you go back and pick them up and coil the empty bine properly.

The measurer was an employee of Whitbread's. With the measurer was a bookie. That bookie used to put in his book what you picked, and then he'd mark it on your card. So you had a record of what you picked, and they had a record. If you lost your card, you'd just have to tell them and you'd get a new one. But it wasn't very often they were lost, I think the women guarded them.

You found a lot of the husbands took their holidays at that time, if they got holidays, and picked with you because that earned you more money and it was a bit of a holiday for the husband. Also the husband could be employed on what they called a pole puller's job. What they did, they had a long pole with a hook on it. Often when you pulled a bine down – because they're strung on wires, overhead – you'd leave the head of it up. You'd call out, "Heads up," and the pole puller'd come out and unhook the head. Or sometimes they would help you with bins when you had to move them to another place. Normally you did it all yourself. Pole pullers would get paid a wage from Whitbread's. Sometimes men from London who were unemployed would come down and work for the season.

You'd get somebody start a song and everybody would be singing. It was lovely ... All the songs of the day. "They try to tell us were're too young." Sometimes they'd sing the old songs. Not "Daisy, Daisy." But of that era. The most popular hopping song was,

"When you go down hopping
Hopping down in Kent
See your Mother Riley
Sitting in a tent.
With a te-i-o, and a te-i-o,
A te-i, e-i-o.

Some say hopping's lousy
You don't believe it's true
We only go down hopping
To earn a bob or two.

You'd sing that as you went onto the field. That was the hopping song.

Kathleen Ash

ALL WEATHERS

In bad weather we still had to pick, but if it got really bad you had to go home, and just sit in the hut chatting, talking, laughing. It was never boring. Lots to do. You couldn't stop long for the rain; you didn't get paid. But hopping would be extended if there was a lot of bad weather. You might get another week out of it. Another week off school! Terrible really.

Elaine Jones

And then, you see, people fainted because the sun was so hot and the humidity and fumes from the hops between the rows got so strong and then, of course, there was always somebody there with the Red Cross on their arm and they called for them and they came along and put sal volatile under their nose – smelling salts. We always took smelling salts with us when we went. My gran used to say, "Get my smelling salts off the dressing table". Because somebody was going to faint. I think it must have been getting in a closed area with the hops because they're about ten or twelve feet high.

Joan Miller

We were looked after at Whitbread's, we really were but you worked for it. It wasn't hard work for me but it's monotonous and tedious. Because all you do is, you pull a bine down, and you put it over your bin and then you pick. And you pick. And you pick. And you swing that bine away and then you pull another down. And you get your leaves out as much as you can. Especially the big ones. What you could do was you sent one of the kids down the line a little bit and they would pick all these branches, the lower branches of the heel, because the kids had time to pick completely clean. So you put the clean ones all on top of yours, so the load looked lovely. I don't suppose the measurers were fooled for a moment! You used to get roughly three measures a day. Sometimes if the oasts were full it would only be two, and you'd grumble like mad, but you'd have to leave those in the bin until the next day. They used to sink overnight with the dew on them, so the next day when you went there you spent some time, whoosh, getting the air in them again and pulling them up so the bin would look fuller.

Kathleen Ash

The measurer was really the overseer. He was in charge. And all the pole pullers, they were like foremen, and they used to work underneath the measurers. And we all used to work under the pole pullers. In my time, they was always men, but in the first war they took on women pole pullers, because there were no men about. My husband was a pole puller. He was at the beck and call of the measurers to help them. He used to have to make sure all the heads was off of the tops of the hop bines, make sure people were comfortable and make sure their bins was moved, see everything's done right.

I was picking hops. The bins were supplied by the farmer. They was so big you could sit on the wooden sides of them, like a bath, and you couldn't fill them up. You'd have twelve bins to a set, right along the alley. My husband used to help me with my bin, he'd pick with me. But he used to hop it when they said, "The measurer's coming round", because the pole pullers were supposed to be making sure everyone was all right and to be helping the measurer to measure the hops out. The measurer knew what he was up to and he used to come up to me sometimes and say "Nell, is this John's bin?" I'd say, "Yeah." He'd say, "Well clean it out then!" You had to clean all the leaves out. Oh, my husband was a dirty picker. Good job I was clean. If they found too many leaves in, they wouldn't take them; you'd have to clean them out first.

As the man came round measuring, he'd got an office girl with him. They used to enter in a measurement in your card, and a date; then at the end of the season, they'd reckon it all up, and that's what you'd got to come back. But you never got paid weekly; you used to have a sub, Tuesdays, Thursdays and Saturdays. If they paid you weekly, you'd either spend it all out, or you might go home, mightn't you! So we used to have what you'd call a sub. Used to have enough to see us over, Saturday to Tuesday, Tuesday to Thursday. We never had much to take home at the end, but we had a cheap holiday. A fine holiday.

Ellen Russell

Mrs Emily Rothery (known as Red Emma of Southwark) 1937 (lent by her daughter, Nell Mason)

You didn't stop, otherwise you didn't earn any money. We worked from half past seven to five o'clock, with a break for lunch. You had what they called a heel – four bines on each heel. You'd have to finish that heel before moving on or stopping for lunch. It was day work and you were paid by results. You could be up there all day and not earn a penny if you didn't work. You had a bin that weighed about three quarter hundredweight, and someone's got to carry that, sometimes half a mile to the next field. If your husband ain't there, you had to carry that bin yourself. Some farms did carry them up for you on the wagon, but nine out of ten times, the wagon would go without you.

You still went out on rainy days because you'd got to earn your living. Leave the kids in the huts and go up there with macs on, get picking. Otherwise you got no money.

Bet Easterbrook

Lunch time at the bin (photo of her mother lent by Eileen Jones)

37

LUNCH BREAK

Once you were on that field you did exactly what the overseer said. It was very regimented because otherwise they couldn't have controlled the crowd that was there. They used to have wooden whistles. When they whistled a very, very long blast that was down tools for lunch. Now in the morning you had a break about half-past nine and that was two short whistles.

They used to get their tea out – in bottles, mostly. They used to put hot tea in lemonade bottles. It got quite cool, but then it was warm. And then we'd take, or collect on the way, bottles of lemonade to drink out of the bottle without a cup.

And then lunch time, when the long blast went, everybody stopped. Even though I was young, I remember everybody stopped, because if somebody went on picking, the people round them would tell them off. Because they were taking longer than they should have done. See, it was a close-cut thing – it was piece-work. So if you were working over the clock, you were doing something you shouldn't have done. So everybody stopped immediately. And then they went into their little circles and some of them went back to the huts. If it was too far they didn't go. We sat down on the ground on a coat or something we'd taken and ate enormous piles of sandwiches.

Kit, Frances and Danny O'Connell take a lunch break with friends

And we used to pick plums or fruit on the way down to the fields and of course the wasps started coming as soon as the Victoria plums were eaten. Then we were stung by wasps and then somebody would have a blue bag (they'd always got things with them) and you'd put the blue bag on it and run around with a blue leg. Wet them and then we'd have blue on our faces!

When it came to lunch time, a man used to come round on his bike blowing a trumpet and that was the signal for the lunch break. My mum used to do up sandwiches and food and that to take out to the fields, so it was like a picnic everyday. The food was wonderful. But if we'd been picking hops, it used to get on the sandwiches. You see, if you've been picking hops, your hands get sort of green and then black, and they smell of hops. And my mum used to tear a piece of paper off the paper bag for us to hold our sandwiches with. My gran used to think we was dreadfully fastidious! She used to say to mum, "They're too fussy."
Joan Clarkson

Ethel Neighbour and her mother at the bin

The whistle would shrill again – a short blast – and they all started immediately. Some of them would have dress watches – there were no wrist watches in those days – and they'd know that the time was coming up. In the field that we used to do, they stopped at four o'clock because they started early at six o'clock in the morning.
Joan Miller

When I was a kid down hopping, the bloke used to come round with rock cakes, doughnuts or bamburys. You could just hear him calling across the field. The old lady would always say "Go and get one of his rock cakes." But if it was raining, they'd all fall to pieces before you could eat them – did I cry then!
Tom Easterbrook

THE POLE PULLER AND THE LONG JOURNEY

Nothing was wasted. If any part of the bine broke at the top the pole pullers would go round and hook it down and drop it into your bin. The pole pullers would also load the pokes onto the wagons, as part of their jobs. They were big sacks, like great long sausages, the pokes. They used to fill them up, tie up the ears of the sacks with cords, lay the poke down, and then when the old cart came along, they'd just throw them up, stack the cart up right high and take them down the kiln for drying. The local people were pole pullers because it was a yearly job for them. They dried all the hops that were picked in September throughout the year. Then they used to come up to London to the hop exchange, because the brewery wanted so many hops. They'd go through the hop exchange and they would auction the hops. You got so many pokes down Bodiam, so many pokes down Frimley, and so many pokes somewhere else ready for sale. Take them up to London and put them in warehouses at Crucifix Lane.

All round the wharves were the warehouses where they used to store the hops. After they'd been dried, they were put into bigger sacks, longer sacks. And they were brought up to London and put in the warehouses at London Bridge. You could smell the hops as you walked past. Some of the hop warehouses are still there. And the hop exchange is still there at London Bridge – in Southwark Street. The hops from all round the country all come to

Minnie Martin with her mother and a handsome pole puller

Louise Hart (photo lent by her daughter, Eileen O'Sullivan)

London on the train. The trains used to run along the one side of the Bricklayers Arms and on the other side they would have a train with a long wagon with all the pokes in. The LMS Railway carts used to go in there and pick them up and take them on to London Bridge.

We had all the breweries round here. Courage's – that was at Tower Bridge ... Whitbread's – they were all round in the docks area. You used to see them arrive on the horse and cart in those days before they started using the trains to carry the hop sacks. When they unloaded the hops from the carts, they had to pick them up by the ears rather than use hooks. Because once you got the air into the pokes it turned the hops if they were stood at the warehouse for a long time. They might go bad, so they had to be kept airtight in hessian sacks.

Bill O'Sullivan

OUR LOVELY HOPS

Beers are all different, some are stronger, like a Guinness, and some are milder, lighter. There would be different hops for different beers. The hops themselves would be different shapes. Some are little bulbous ones, some are long, like a pear – you get different varieties. And the smell! Not just the hops but the leaves themselves, if you rub them, the smell's really strong. You go through a hop field of a morning – its beautiful! With the smell of the hops and the dew, the fresh dew!

Flo Batley

WHITBREAD & CO., LTD.,

BELTRING, PADDOCK WOOD, KENT.

HOP-PICKING.

RULES AND REGULATIONS TO BE OBSERVED BY BINMEN.

1. Binmen must be in the Hop Gardens at 7 a.m.

2. They must provide a constant supply of bines for six bins. All bines must be cut by the Binmen at the top wires, and none should on any account be pulled down, either by the Binmen or the Pickers. All tops, or branches, left on the wires after the bine has been cut down must be taken down at once, and not allowed to hang and wither.

3. Binmen are responsible for seeing that the ground is cleared of dropped hops, and pickers should not be allowed to trample hops underfoot.

4 Binmen must look after their pickers, and see that they pick the hops cleanly and free from bunches. All hops must be picked from the bines, unless the Hop-garden Manager orders otherwise. When finished with, the picked bines should be wound neatly round the hill stumps.

5. Binmen must carry out their full pokes and load them on to the wagons immediately after each measuring. They must not put them down and leave them. No child or boy is to be allowed to fetch or carry pokes, either empty or full.

6. Binmen must be particularly careful to see that 10 bushels of hops, neither more nor less, are put into each poke. They should see that the pokes for the night loadings are tied loosely.

7. When taking up fresh ground, a Binman should see that all the members of his Company move together.

8. Each Binman is responsible for his pokes, knife, lapbag and bincloths.

9 No Binman may on any account take the pokes of another, without first having obtained permission from the Hop-garden Manager, or his Assistants.

10. Binmen must immediately report anyone breaking the rules, stealing or doing wilful damage in any part of the farm.

11. No Binman may leave the Hop Gardens during working hours, without special permission.

12 Binmen's wages are fixed at............per day for each completed working day, which may, if desired. be subbed on the usual days. Binmen are engaged by the day, and may be dismissed at any time without notice. An additional sum of 6d, per working day will be paid to each Binman who is not discharged for unsatisfactory conduct, and remains throughout the picking.

Special Notice.

In the past we have found some Binmen have been inclined to neglect their proper work to pick hops. We wish all Binmen clearly to understand that they are allowed to pick as a favour, and only on the strict understanding that such picking does not interfere with any of their proper duties.

Daphne Wallace's father (Albert Slack) and family

A HOME-DWELLER'S VIEW

My parents lived in a tied cottage on a farm where there was hops. My father used to be the measurer during the hopping season and that meant that he was more or less in charge of the hop fields. I remember from quite an early age, I don't know how old I was, we used to get up early and he used to go round the huts, or the common as they used to call it, and knock people up in the mornings, because in those days you had to be out in the hop field at seven o'clock. He just used to bang on the door.

They have to get so many pokes of hops each day to put in the kilns to dry them. And often if you weren't out there very early in the morning, then to get the number of hops they required you had to be out there until about six o'clock at night. He didn't have anything to do with the drying of the hops, but he had to make sure they got enough hops to dry, depending how many kilns they had.

It used to be very long hours, late hours. It could be six or seven o'clock before they'd measured all the hops. After he'd measured them, there'd be a tally man with him, noting how many bushels someone had picked, and that was put down on their card. It was also written into a large book by the measurer because on these big places there used to be a hundred bins or more.

The hop-pickers used to have a little hut place where the farm manager would pay out subs on Tuesdays, Thursdays and Saturdays, or something like that.

I used to sometimes go up to the huts with my father if there had been a wet day. They never used to really pick when it was raining hard. But if in the morning it was too wet to pick, and about ten o'clock it had left off, then my father used to have to go round the huts and shout, "Get out in the hop fields." Well then I used to go with him.

I remember when the hop-pickers went on strike. They had to pick seven bushels for a shilling, and then they had it reduced down to six bushels a shilling. That was about the 1930s. I wasn't very old.

I know it used to very awkward for him in the pub. The hop-pickers used to have their own rooms, but my father used to like to drink at weekends, Sunday lunchtime, Sunday nights, Saturday nights. And as he went down to the pub, there would be several Londoners wanting to buy him a drink, but he would never accept a drink from them, not while he was working with them, because somebody would say, "Oh yes, I bought you a pint at the weekend, count them a bit light for me," and that sort of thing. You have a rim round the basket you see, and there's a knack of it, where you just flick the hops around in the basket, so it looks fuller than it is. But my father never used to get involved socially with the Londoners, or at least not until the day they went back. When the hops were finished, they would be paid the next day. Well, the next day, he'd meet them in the pub and he'd have a drink to be sociable with everyone.

Daphne Wallace

YOUNG HOPPERS

ON THE FIELDS

There were young babies in their prams on the field. They'd tuck those children in and push them down the far end of the hop field where it's all quiet and leave them. You could rest assured nothing would happen to those babies. And if you went away to do a pee or something like that, you had someone to look after your children. If somebody started singing on the field, everybody joined in, and it was lovely to hear all these people singing.

Marjorie Balcombe

They'd stick babies in a pram or a box, sometimes an upturned apple box. Some of the toddlers had a string from the hops round their waist and the other end tied to the end of the hop bin, so their parents could keep an eye on them.

Elaine Jones

We used to love hop-picking. We used to pick for Mum and Dad during the week and on Friday you used to pick for yourself, so you could go into Maidstone on the Saturday and buy whatever you wanted.

Albert Bowers

I was about nine years old the first time we went hop-picking. They used to open umbrellas for the children to fill with hops. Pick so many and you got pocket money. And then we used to have a van come round during the day, selling sweets or fried fish. You'd get good food down there, you had enough to eat. I don't know if it was the fresh air that did it, but you were always eating – we'd put on weight by the time we come home!

Vi Lewis

I liked picking the hops. I was never a great one for mixing, although I was used to being with cousins and aunties at Nan's house at weekends. Nan had thirteen children. And like all London families, where Nan was, all the family were. All the aunts got married and they all had their kids upstairs in the front bedroom. I wasn't one of the in-crowd of the cousins. They would lark, run around the house. I'd never run around Nan's house. Too shy. And when we went hopping, I enjoyed the picking, whereas probably the rest of the cousins enjoyed running over the fields, and scrumping and all that sort of thing. I was with grandmother and life was quiet. I enjoyed the picking; the blacker my hands got the more I liked it. The only time Nan used to shout was when the tally man used to come round. When he was on his way round, it was, "Come on you kids, out the way." Out would come the leaves, we'd pick all the leaves out, ready for the man with the basket.

Lilian Carter

To be quite honest, I didn't like hop-picking. I never did. I was an only daughter, and I think I was pampered, I didn't like the rough and tumble of it. I didn't like the feel of the bines on my hands, the roughness. I would rather stay in the hut and tidy the hut than go up to the fields. My mother was from a big family, nine in her family. They all went hop-picking and they really had a good old time of it. In those days, they went all the way from Bermondsey to Paddock Wood on a horse and cart and it took them two and a half days to get there. When they were going up hill, the children would have to get out and walk at the side of the cart. My father was working in the docks and he came down on the Friday night. I used to wait for him to come down, and Saturday he'd take me for a walk. We'd go through the orchards to Marden village. But the weekdays I didn't enjoy one bit.

Eileen O'Sullivan

Susan Wallace (photo lent by Daphne Wallace)

When I was very young, our family used to go to Hawkhurst for hop-picking. But when I was a teenager, abut fifteen years of age, we went to Five Oak Green, Paddock Wood. My mum always said, if I never went hop-picking, she wouldn't, because I was her mainstay, I did everything for her. I used to get up very early in the morning to go down the hop field. We'd take chairs and all sorts with us. It used to be very cold to start with, the mist used to be like a fog and all the hops would be wringing wet! If you got a mist like that, you knew you were in for a lovely day when the sun came out. My mum used to stay behind, she'd cut up the sandwiches for the lunch, make a big pot of tea and then she'd bring it up the field, so we could have a little break. We had everything in the field – breakfast, dinner, dirt and everything!

My brother never liked hop-picking, he used to stand there in a dream. And I used to get mad at him, because I was working hard, why shouldn't he? I said to him, "Why don't you pick quick and earn some money?" He said, "I am picking quick!" I said, "You're not! All you're doing is standing there singing." He said, "Well, I'm picking to my singing." So I said, "Well, sing a quick song then!" My mum never forgot that, she laughed her head off.

Minnie Martin

In the morning the kids would go down and they'd congregate at Gran's bin. And it's, "Now come on you lot, make a start. Come on, give your nan a start." And then you'd have one bine and about three kids on it, and they're pulling it off. "Not like that, like this!" 'Course they all put everything in, the leaves and all, don't they?

Ethel Neighbour

photo lent by Minnie Martin

photo lent by Mike Fitzgerald

LOLLY MAN

A bloke used to come on a bike with a basket on, and sweets and bits and pieces whatever he had. And they'd see him coming along the road, "Lolly man!" all the kids yelled out. "Quick mum, there's the lolly man." Some mothers would say, "You don't pick no bleedin' hops, you'll get no money from me!" Then the kid'd come over, "Can you lend my mummy tuppence for the lolly man?" "Give her tuppence for the lollyman, we'll give it to you tonight." Probably my kids would say, "Lolly man, Mum, can I have some money?" She'd say, "Oh, how many hops you pick?" "Three." "Should've picked ten, then you'd get a lolly. You pick the ten, you get thruppence."

Mike Fitzgerald

The kids would run away if they could. The kids never liked picking that much – sometimes you'd say to them, "Come and pick for me for a little while and I'll buy you a lolly." That was a sweet lolly – not an ice cream.

Kathleen Ash

We used to pray for rain as kids. There was this huge bin, and we used to have to fill it up with hops. Even when it rained my mother and grandmother would still carry on, but we wouldn't, we stopped. Under the end of the bin, my mother would put down sacks to make a sort of tent and we used to get in there out of the way of the rain. We used to pray for rain so we could get away! We used to play football in the evenings and they used to have these magic lantern shows in the field for the children. I remember we used to like going along to watch the pigs in the field nearby.

Bob Bennett

We hated the actual picking, as children. "We hate picking! We're never coming helping again first thing in the morning!" The bines were wringing wet, the drips would all run down your neck. And the insects, I hated bugs! When I got into bed, I'd cover my ears up because of the earwigs – I always thought that they were called earwigs because they climbed into your ears. If it was raining, we didn't go picking. We'd go down the cookhouse and roast potatoes or apples on the fire. You put the apples on a stick to roast them – you always had your sticks with your name carved on it. If it was wet all day long we used to play games indoors like "I spy". We'd put on a show, and dance.

Joyce Berry

The year my youngest son Chrissie was born was the first year I missed going hopping. That was because he was born right in the middle of the hop-picking season, 16th September, 1947. The next year was the first year Chrissy went. And he went up until he was about ten years old. I always used to maintain that it built him up for the winter. I felt very strongly about it.

The kids used to go running round the fields and on the common, playing football, but they never really got into mischief. Say the kids had picked in the morning, you'd let them off in the afternoon. You used to say to them, "Now, you pick here for an hour. And then when you've had your lunch, you can go and play." Did they work? Cor, you got more work out of them in that hour than you could have got out of them all day! They'd run off, but I would know where to find them. They'd be on the common, or back at the huts. When you got back from work, they'd be there.

"Now you kids pick here for an hour!" (photo lent by Ellen Russell)

In our family, we had my young sister-in-law, my husband's sister. She used to stop behind Saturday mornings – she never went out working Saturday – and she used to wash the kids for us, plenty of hot water, and get a cup of tea ready for us when we come off the field, twelve o'clock. And then we'd be on the van, up the town shopping.

We always used to have my son's birthday on the hop fields. I've got some photographs of that, and you'd be surprised how good they are, only little tiny things from a Woolworths camera. Everybody used to bring out tables and table cloths and plates and cups and saucers, everything; even flower vases. We used to buy flowers as well. And we'd line all the tables up along the common, all along by the huts. And we used to invite all the kids. Everyone came to Chris's birthday party. Then the grown ups always had a party after Chris's birthday.

Ellen Russell

Chris Russell's birthday party (photo lent by Ellen Russell)

SCRUMPING

By today's standards, what the kids did wasn't very much. You never got huts broken into, and there must have been things in there that would have been of value to someone. Children did go into the orchards, getting the apples and all that; scrumping. You'd get the farmer come round and find out who it was. But parents were pretty strict on their kids, because they were so frightened that their children were going to get them into trouble and they wouldn't be able to come hopping any more. So the children would probably get a wallop if it was found that they were scrumping. But then on the other hand I can always remember eating lots of apples. I'm sure we didn't pay for them!

Elaine Jones

As children we used to go scrumping. We'd go for walks in country lanes to look around and see what was what. All of a sudden, you'd hear a cry go up, "The lolly man's here!" And we'd all run back to the field and say, "Mum, I want a lolly". In one field there was a ditch filled with water and over the other side was beautiful apple trees. So when no-one was looking we went across there and threw the apples down. On our way home from the hop field, we used to come down this little lane belonging to the farmer, and there were these big haystacks and all the chickens used to run around. Well, we knew that they used to go under the haystack and lay their eggs, so of course, being children, we used to put our hands under and see if there was any eggs under there. So we had eggs for breakfast, dinner and tea. My mother wouldn't say, "take them back," put it that way, because the farmer didn't miss them.

Florence Burgess

Babies in the hop fields (photo lent by Albert Bowers)

Mike Rothery with full pockets? (photo lent by Nell Mason)

My daughter used to go scrumping, her and her mates. She knew where all the best trees were, right in the middle of the orchard. She'd take a couple of mates with her, see her climb up the tree and take the apples. She done it one night, she's up the tree; all of a sudden the farmer's son come along and said, "Right. Caught you. Got you. I'm telling your dad about you."

Then when she wasn't well in the huts one week, the farmer came down and brought her some soup and some sweets. He said, "I've saved so many pounds of apples this week!"

Mike Fitzgerald

There were miles of kids; no-one worried where they were. We'd be out all day. No fear of being mugged or molested. Miles of kids at all the different farms.

Anne Fitzgerald

I do remember once, a young girl got pulled up by a farmer for scrumping in an orchard, and we pleaded with him, not charge her. I think he did it to frighten her. It was at one of the fruit farms we had to walk through as a right of way to go to Ulcombe. And we were going through his orchard – it was a right of way, we were entitled to. I suppose he was watching. She pinched an apple. And in the end we gave him five shillings. On reflection I think he did act to frighten not only her but us as well.

Harry Demarne

We got caught scrumping. The farmer caught me and my sister and a gang of about fourteen of us. He took our names and addresss and he prosecuted us. My sister and I were too young to appear in court, so my mother had to go. She got fined £5 each for the two of us and she had to pay that £10 on the day she appeared.

All the children went scrumping though ... The parents used to go in the pub and have a drink on the Saturday night, and all the kids were left alone, so we hopped off – scrumping!

Peg King

We'd go scrumping. We'd take the pram and probably a pramload of tiny kids all holding on. We'd be up the apple tree or the plum tree, and we knew the farmer and his wife would be up the fields. We'd fill the prams up with the apples, come back about five hours later. We'd say, "We'll go back and get the kettle on, and the fire going for me mum." We even used to go on the train lines. To get back to the farm, we had to walk over train lines. The poor little kids we had with us would be bit by earwigs, and weeing and everything, and the nappies would be ringing wet, the mum's would all be going; "There they are!" We'd all get a wallop, being out all day.

My neighbourhood friend, Ali, her mum had sixteen kids and no father. Poor mother. They all used to go up the field, the mother'd get a big loaf of bread, be cutting it there as she stood, bit of pilchards on or dripping or whatever. She and her mother never even had time to go to the toilet, she used to stand and go at the bin! She used to stand and do it as she spoke to you, didn't she? I don't know how! Makes you wonder.

There used to be a toilet. And there'd be about six seats cut out, and everybody'd sit on there together!

Anne Fitzgerald

Pramloads of tiny kids 1930s
(photo lent by Whitbread Hop Farm)

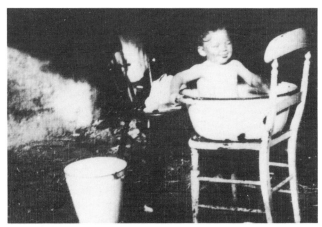

Baby Kathleen at bath time (photo lent by Kathleen Ash)

While the grown-ups picked, the youngsters played. A group of us wandered away and my cousin, Patty, fell down a well. It couldn't have been very deep because I don't remember being scared. Eventually, one of the bigger boys managed to get her out. We used to wander through the orchards, scrumping apples which we carried in the skirts of our dresses. We rarely brought any back as someone would always shout, "Here comes the farmer!" and we'd drop them in our haste to escape.

The things I most remember are the way the straw would be so sharp at night and by the morning would be beautifully soft, and then the absolute thrill of being grown-up enough, at about seven years of age to pull down the first hop-bine, totally unaided.

The huts that we lived on consisted of a long row of huts, each divided in two, so that the rooms backed on to each other. I can't remember if they were detached.

There was a tiny hole in the adjoining wall and when I was a very little girl, I remember lying in bed, peering through the hole. I could see my aunt Dolly, uncle Charlie, and my cousin Charlie, the same age as me. Uncle Charlie was dad's brother. I could see Charlie using the potty. I thought I was very rude and didn't tell anyone that I had seen him!

Jean Simmer

I was one of the older children down there – Mum would leave me behind if one of the other kids weren't well, or she wanted any extra shopping done. We'd go scrumping ... if we passed any plum trees, we'd get a few plums. I think the farmer must have known. When that Mr Dawes came round on his white horse, he would shout and bawl at you and push you back to the field; "You've not been brought down here for a bloody holiday, you get back and do your work; that's what you're paid to come down here for!"

When we pulled the bines down, we'd roll them up and put them at the end of the alley way. Sometimes a mother would put a blanket over that, and lay her baby on it, underneath the shade of the hop bines. It was lovely and healthy for babies, at least that's what we were told anyway. And if the other children were tired in the afternoon, they used to have to go down there as well and lie down.

Laura Murphy

"We used to pray for rain as kids" (photo, 1930s, lent by Whitbread Hop Farm)

It was a good holiday for children. It was the only holiday that was available to us. People used to come from Bethnal Green, all over, to go hop-picking. You'd meet people at London Bridge you'd never seen for a year. There wasn't many letters in those days and there was no telephone. So you didn't see people until the following year until you met them again when they opened their hut door and you opened your hut door and the same people would be there.

The only part about hop-picking I didn't like was the very heavy dews – they would come down like a wet mist of a night-time. The dew would cover everything, inside the hut as well. I hated putting on wet clothes of a morning!

We had the big hobnail boots and socks, and these short trousers. When we were down hopping, we used to sneak away to go fishing. We used to catch eels. They were fascinating to get because they used to twist round your arm. But accidents happened when you were fishing! You get one boy standing there fishing, put his hook in with a piece of bread on the end, and he'd say, "Oh, got one, I've got one." Before you know where you are, everybody's rushing down to have a look and pushing behind you and the first boy's in the water! And you've got boots and socks and trousers on, and sometimes it was cold. You had no chance. Mud and grass is very slippery with those boots on and in you'd go. There was always someone falling in the river.

Bill O'Sullivan

The chickens used to run all round the farm, and lay their eggs. So if you saw an egg, you'd pick it up ... if you didn't pick it up somebody else would. If a kid had picked an egg up, they knew they mustn't tell anyone, they'd come back and give it to Mum and whisper, "I found an egg". One particular time, my young sister was only about four or five. She came back to where all the mums were sitting round the field, all picking the hops and said "Mum! I found an egg and it didn't even break!" She'd found an egg that they'd put there to encourage chickens to lay. And all she could think of was, "It didn't even break."

Laura Murphy

We used to have the Salvation Army come round, and give the children a magic lantern show. We used to sit there glued to this little magic thing. They'd put a big white sheet up in the cookhouse and you would all sit round. They used to have like a policeman's torch behind it, used to shine the light through onto the screen.

Bill O'Sullivan

My mother and grandmother liked a drink. We used to sit outside the pub with a lemonade or arrowroot or something like that and we played. All the pubs in those days had a little room where children could go if they didn't want to wait outside.

Bob Bennett

My dog always used to catch rabbits and bring them home dead. This day, I stayed at the huts and the rest of the family was all at the fields. My dog came along and laid this little thing at my feet, I thought it was a dead bird – it was wringing wet, and then when I looked, it was a tiny baby rabbit. Anyway I dried the rabbit and we keep it for about two or three weeks. Someone made the hutch for it. Every night we used to bring the rabbit in because it got so cold out there. Well this night, we forgot to bring the rabbit in. I went out there the next morning and it was stiff! Well I went mad, because I loved animals! I wrapped it all up and sat round the cookhouse all the next day, nursing it. I didn't go hop-picking. But that rabbit was so stiff it slipped through the blanket and fell on its head. I saw it give a last little wince – oh I'd killed it! When my Mum came home, I wouldn't let her in the hut, I was crying on the bed.

But the funeral we had for that rabbit! We had it laid out on this plank of wood with all flowers round it. And all us younger kids marched up to what we called "the jungle", it was a wood just past the hop field. So we all shed tears and we buried it out in the jungle. We had a cross, and laid all the little flowers on the rabbit's grave.

Barbara Fitzgerald

On top of the world (photo lent by Albert Bowers)

If you were hop-picking at Hawkhurst, you're not far from Hastings. One Sunday, the farmer's wife said, "Come on, we'll all get a bus and go to Hastings." My little boy was only about three years old, he'd never seen the sea. He took one look at the waves and said, "Cor mum, what a big bath!"

Minnie Martin

Kids playing at weddings on Lily Farm (photo lent by Mike Fitzgerald)

Kit O'Connell picking with daughter Frances (left), son Danny, and Susan Wallace

BACK TO SCHOOL

We always used to get in trouble going back to school, because we used to play truant and the teacher used to be after us. You weren't supposed to go hopping because school started in September. When you came back to London, you were covered with hop stain, all over your hands. You could rub it off, like the way you use a rubber, but that black stain would be all over your hands. It'd take at least three weeks from when you came home to get it all off. You couldn't tell your teacher you hadn't been hop-picking, because with a nun that would be a sin. "Where have you been Billy?" "Hopping, miss." "Well you know you're not supposed to go, don't you?" It didn't really bother us. Hop-picking was a holiday so we looked forward to it. So you took the consequences when you come home. Mum would go up to the teacher and say, "We had to go hopping because we need the money." The teacher would say, "Don't do it no more." Then next year it'd be the same.

Bill O'Sullivan

My mother was in a state! She was faced with a type-written official letter with the school rules listed on it. She was concentrating on the section headed "Uniform". "If hair is straight it must be plaited, tied back or cut above the collar. On no account is hair allowed to be put up or artificially curled". My hair was straight and just on the collar, so she frantically squeezed and pulled my little bit of hair into two plaits, bound each one of them tightly with rubber bands and added massive brown bows to each of them. On top of this was to go the brand new school beret, flat as a pancake with a heavy metal badge with SERVIAM written on it.

So off I went thinking that I looked quite wonderful with a school tunic and mac, nearly down to my ankles so that it would last, a brand new heavy leather satchel, pencil box, fountain pen, in fact everything new, including big brown knickers. What a sight I must have looked, but I was bursting with pride as I opened the door into the classroom – ten days later, than all the other girls, because we had been hop-picking.

I was faced with the poshest person I had ever encountered, a Nun reported to have been French aristocracy before she entered the convent. She said to me with very pronounced whssss, "Where have you been?" "Dahn 'Oppin'", I replied, "Where?", she repeated. "Dahn 'Oppin'", I repeated. This went on for ages until she finally said "Doo yoo mean hop-picking?" "Yeh" I said. "Oh go and sit down child" she uttered with disgust. My heart sank. What on earth was she on about? for the first time in my life I was aware that "going hoppin" was anything but good.

Frances O'Connell

50

YOUNG HOME-DWELLERS

The local school holidays were more or less timed with when the hops were ready. We never used to break up until the end of August then. Kids like us were sent up the front of the row and we used to pick the hops into an upturned umbrella. Funnily enough, we didn't meet a lot of the London kids. They had to work during the day. That's all they came down there for, to get their clothes for the next school term. We locals just never seemed to meet them. All the locals had their own sets of hops, and the Londoners had theirs. For some reason you wasn't integrated at all.

At that time also there was large bushes of blackberries, and all of the local kids went picking those. Just down the road here at New Farm, there must have been forty or fifty acres of blackberries there. We picked them for Smedleys, the jam firm which is near Maidstone. So it wasn't just hop-picking. And then you got the main crop of apples at the same time. My mother very seldom went hop-picking; she always went apple-picking, blackberries, plums. You hardly see plums now, but there were acres and acres of plums in those days. Even cob nuts.

Bill Slack

The Seadon children picking in the 1930s
(photo lent by Dot Seadon)

Brother Sydney aged 6 years (Minnie Martin)

Children are apt to put leaves in so they weren't encouraged to pick many. So most of the time we ran round the fields and played with the children who came down from London. A lot of them had bare feet. They weren't encouraged to wear shoes down there in the mud, so they didn't have any, so of course they used to like to try our shoes on and sometimes we used to lose our shoes because they took them! They were cuter than us, don't forget – they had to be.

But we used to run up and down the lines, getting in everybody's way and being told off. It was all fun, though. Nobody ever got really mad about it because the people there seemed to love children – they all had children, all big families. If there was any swearing I didn't hear it, or I didn't notice it. My mother told me there wasn't an awful lot of swearing in those days in front of children. Not a lot. The odd word. Not all the time. They seemed to be able to keep that for the publichouse or somewhere else. But we really enjoyed ourselves.

Joan Miller

COOKING

Cooking on wood fires at Whitbread's

We used to pick all day and in the evening, Mum used to cook the dinner ... mostly stew. The people who used to live down there – homedwellers, we'd call them, they used to come round and sell rabbits. I think they were about sixpence or a shilling each. Mum would cut them up and make a rabbit stew, put a belly of pork in it, and it used to be lovely. My mum used to be a cook before she got married so we had good food, we were lucky. But we did have good food down there. And plenty of vegetables. Vegetables were cheap down there.

Laura Murphy

The others would be working during the day but some of the older women used to stay behind with us kids and peel potatoes with us. We used to do a lot of little chores like that to help get a meal ready in the evening for when the hop-pickers came back. The food there was better than what we got in town. It was fresh milk from the cow. A lot of youngsters had never seen vegetables growing before, never knew that they dug up potatoes from the ground.

Bill Webb

Our main meals were almost always stews, which tasted gorgeous, either sausage stews, just sausages, onions and potatoes, or mutton stews. My favourite meal is still a stew.

On Sundays we would have a leg of pork or lamb (meat was cheap in those days). We used to take it to the local baker who cooked it for us for 6d.

Tom Baldwin

You were allowed so many faggots for your fires. You had to be careful with it and use it at the right time. You had hopping pots to cook in, big round cooking pots. You'd have a pot hanging over the fire for boiling puddings. You'd put it on there when you went off to work. It was put in a muslin; a steak and kidney pudding or a suet pudding with fruit in, any pudding. And you'd put it in the water. I don't know why it didn't get all wet, but it come out all shiny and lovely, very appetising. We did custard or syrup over it. Or just sugar. We had enamel plates. We took cutlery from home, we took everything.

Flo Batley

We stopped work at six or seven o'clock in the evening. Normally me and my sister were sent home early to get the dinner cooking. It was mostly stew or meat pudding or a big piece of bacon that would last a long time. We would boil it over a fire outside the hut. One day my brother was cooking some sausages over the fire and he'd done one load and put them in the plate and then came into the hop hut to get the rest of the sausages. Meanwhile, a loose dog stole all the sausages that he'd cooked. I remember him chasing the dog around.

We would get the vegetables from the farmer who was very good to my mum. The country people were always good to my mum. Some people say that there was a lot of tension between the London hop-pickers and the locals, but that wasn't my experience. Not where I went.

Kit O'Connell

We were out picking on the field at seven in the morning. My mother used to say to me, "Right, you can stay behind and make the beds. Do the potatoes for tonight, do this for tonight, do that for tonight." There wasn't a lot of cooking done because we never had a lot of facilities. We had like a camp fire outside, like the boy scouts have. The bar across and the two bits down, and the hook that you hang your pots on. You could do that outside your hut until it rained. Then there was one particular hut that was made into what they called the cookhouse. This was set up with bars across all round to cook your dinner on. Everyone had the same, it was all boiled – everything all in the pot together. Anything. Dumplings, vegetables. But we always looked after each other if you got someone that wasn't well. We all knew each other by our first names.

Marjorie Balcombe

Mostly you could only boil food, everything was boiled on the camp fire. It was all nourishing fresh food. They would cook boiled bacon – buy a big lump of bacon. Salt beef. Stews. Everybody had stews. You could put roast potatoes in the embers – put them in and while you were cooking the rest of your meal, the potatoes would be cooking. Some of the grandmothers when we used to go round on Sundays could really cook good food on those fires. My mother used to do a pot roast. You have a big pot – we've got one in the garden shed now – big iron pot. And they put their joint of meat in the pot, with fat – like deep fried – and they'd put that in the embers and slowly cook it and it would roast, and you'd put potatoes in it and they also would roast. You'd do most of your cooking at the weekends and in the evenings. You weren't allowed to go back to the hut during the day. We'd take sandwiches to the fields. Mostly bread and cheese or corned beef. Most people cooked in the evenings. Sausages, you'd have a big pan, and fried food, or you'd have stew with dumplings.

Eileen O'Sullivan

You had faggots, that's bundles of branches, delivered to you and you made your fire. If you built a good hob of bricks you could cook some really good meals. You'd take part of your stove with you, perhaps some of the racks.

Tom Easterbrook tends the fire

You'd take a pan, we used to call it our billy can, and you'd put it on the griddle. You had an old black kettle for boiling. It was amazing how we managed. We used to boil up potatoes, sausages, a bit of bacon.

I used to cook on the fire. You'd build a great big fire, and let it go right down to embers. Then you'd put a grating over that, and this tray on the top, and you're cooking in a saucepan all the time. I used to do mostly the Sunday food. That was the big meal. I used to put a bit of fat in the saucepan, put the joint in – we always had a joint Sundays – and put the lid on top, and then it'd cook itself. It didn't go dry because you've got a bit of fat in it, plus the fat out of the meat, and the potatoes used to go round the side of that.

We used to take my mother-in-law home to the huts sometimes to cook for us, and she'd make a great big currant pudding. We'd send the boys back with her to get the fire going, and my mother-in-law cooked on that open fire. There was always something to eat when we come in off the field. You'd have sausages, mash and onions, all things like that, chops, steaks. In the evenings we used to sit round the old camp fire and have a sing-song, just like the scouts do.

If my mother-in-law was cooking, I'd put the boys to pick on her bin. Someone had to do her hops if she was going to cook their food for them. That's how we used to work it out. Or my husband'd go on her bin. If I was cooking, my husband was there to do my bin for me.

Ellen Russell

After you picked all day, you go home and you really are starving; because the air's marvellous. So the women set about making the tea – stew again!

Outside the huts, you'd do your cooking. Now and again, if you were lucky, you might have a fry-up. But mostly it was stew, stew, stew. There'd be butchers' shops down there in the village; you'd have to walk a couple of mile to the village to get the bit of meat – always the cheapest cuts naturally – and you'd bung that in. Or faggots – we used to have faggot stew ... the cheapest stuff you could think of, we'd eat it; you're hungry, you'd eat anything.

Stanley Rose

I remember once we were out picking in the fields and we were desperate for a cup of tea. I sent my nine-year-old sister-in-law back to the huts to fetch a cup of tea. She'd been gone about two hours and I thought, "Where's she gone?" Eventually she comes across the fields carrying the jug, and when she pours it out, she's forgotten to put the tea in if you please, so it's boiled water. I had to go three fields home again to make a pot of tea.

Flo Batley

On most farms you cooked outside on open fires, but Whitbread's used to provide us with cookhouses. They were brick built with tin roofs, three of them back to back, with three fire places in each and three chimneys. They used to provide us with bundles of firewood from where they trimmed and cleared all the hedges. They used to call them faggots, and they were all tied up with string or wire. We used to cook in the cookhouse, but then the second year we went, it must have been 1938, my mother acquired – I don't remember where from – a double burner oil stove, with an oven on top which she could use in our hut.

My gran would cook us eggs and bacon, things like that, for breakfast. We used to eat very well there. Lunch was things like cheese and corned beef with pickle. We used to love that.

We used to go blackberry-picking, my sister and mum's sister Eileen. We used to go scrumping and my gran would make us a big blackcurrant and apple dumpling. It was big, you know, cooked in a cloth, in a very big saucepan outside on that fire in the cook hut. It was lovely. Every year without fail she did that, and it was the most marvellous treat, because it was absolutely wonderful.

We used to have a butcher's van come round every day to where the huts were. They came down from London in an old van, and either they would sell off the back of the van, or they would have the van altered and have a side panel, that came down. My mum and my gran would buy fresh meat every day. We always had a roast dinner Sunday at a big trestle table. I only remember the weather being good, and Sundays were wonderful.

Joan Clarkson

Outside the huts, to the side would be what they called the cookhouse. Well it'd only be a shed more or less, open all the way round ... just a tin roof on the four legs I suppose ... but there were places where you could build your fires – if it was wet at all you *had* to use this shed! There was a piece of iron along the top and you built your fire underneath that. Then you could put your pots on this S piece of iron and hang your pot up. You'd cook everything on that, and you would push your kettle into the ashes. Sometimes you would burn your fire outside your hut, but they always used to say it was dangerous. But we did it. A lot of people did.

Laura Murphy

You know those big old iron pots? Well my Mother-in-law used to make a lovely spotted dog, for the whole family. She'd boil it in the pot about four hours and it would come out lovely. My brother-in-law, Danny, came back from the hop field one day and he saw the pot on the boil. He went into the hut and got his fork and his plate out, he's gonna be first ain't he? Mother-in-law said, "What are you waiting for, Dan?" He said, "I'm waiting for the pudding to come out." She said, "That's my tea towels I'm boiling!" Two and a half hours he'd been waiting there – we'd all gone up the pub!

Tom Easterbrook

You'd have what they call cook huts. All the families would be in there when it was wet. You'd light a fire and you'd have your meals cooking there. My mum had a lovely stew cooking once, and my brother come along and said, "Mum, what's in that pot you've got on the fire?" She said, "Me stew." He said, "Well it ain't anymore, the little boy up the huts has just peed in it!" She had to throw the whole dinner away but she chased that boy all round the common first. And every time after that we saw him, we'd call out: "Piss in a pot!"

Bet Easterbrook

Dot Seadon and her daughter in the cookhouse

We used to go to Paddock Wood. I can't remember how old I was when I first went down, but I was very young. I really enjoyed it. Especially when they used to put the bars up for the saucepans. You never had a kettle – it was always a saucepan with a lid, hung on a little hook over the fire. The tea was never ever smoky, even with all the smoke coming up around the pot. You used to have the other pot for cooking your meat and stuff on the fire. It seems that we always had lamb strips, pot cooked – not a stew; a baked pot roast they call it. It's very, very nice. You'd put the other vegetables in another pot on the hook hanging over the fire to cook while the roast was on.

Mrs Arundale

COOKHOUSE

The cookhouse was a massive big shed with about five fires in, brick built fires with hooks hanging from them, which people hung their pots from. They lit a fire and all cooked in there. And they had a bench behind it, and you sat there and watched it cook. And in the evening, if it was cold or that, people would actually sit in there, because the fires were still going. You'd go and sit and chat.

Elaine Jones

Harry Fitzgerald and the hopping pot

Aunts Sarah, Kate and Dolly preparing vegetables (photo lent by Mike Fitzgerald)

Traders on the hop field (photo lent by Ellen Russell)

THE FARM SHOP

They'd open up a big barn which was the only shop. I mean, talk about monopoly, because otherwise you had to go right into Tonbridge on a bus. And that'd be opened up for the season, and that was really only a barn, and they'd have it all stocked up with food and that. And the queues, you'd have to queue for ages.

And then the milk used to come from the urns. You'd put your jug out, and you'd say, "Two pints." and he poured it in, and it was straight from the cows, across the field. That Friday night you'd get a fish and chip man come, it really was good business for people.

You'd get chicken people come round selling chickens, and things like that. I don't know where they got them, but nobody asked! There was a lot of poaching. I do remember, this chap. He had a greengrocer's in London, and he used to come down and load his lorry up with apples! On the quiet. And where we lived in Hoxton it was quite notorious really. Next door to us was a chap who'd always been in prison, but he was always escaping. And whenever he did, when he was on the run, he used to come down hopping, it was all hush hush, but that's where he was. But the police used to know, so they'd be down there and asking in the huts if they'd seen him. "Oh no, no, we haven't seen him. He hasn't been down here." But he really wasn't a terribly bad criminal. My nan always says they just picked on him when he was young, so it started with him being put away early, and because he was such a wiry, canny little fellow, he'd get out.

Elaine Jones

On Whitbread's Farm there were stores. There was a greengrocer's, with all fresh produce. There was a store that sold clothes, socks, different things. And there was a provisions tent during the war where you used to take your rations book over, line up and get your rations. There was also a butcher's stall in one of the barns.

My hut was right opposite the tea place which was called Sid's. He used to do hot tea and hot pies and whacking great big cheesecakes! At the end of the day, we came off the field tired and I'd know I'd have to get something going for the dinner. But first, we would get two penn'orth of tea in a jug – a nice lot of tea in a jug. You'd sit and drink that cup of tea and the kids'd have a drop as well, before you got on with the dinner.

If you lit the fire and let it go right down, you could do a little bit of frying. You shared the cookhouse with somebody else and sometimes they had a great big fire as well and you'd get little bits of black flying around. It never spoiled anything – in fact it must have been the first attempts at barbecueing! On Sundays, you could walk about three miles down to the baker's and take your joint and the potatoes and they would bake it. The knack was, you had to go back there at two o'clock to get it and walk back with it. We used to take a pram, put the roast in the pram and cover it over with a cloth. But it would get a little bit cold by the time you got back to the hut. During the week, it was soups, stews, everything was boiled. You'd get a lovely meal out of boiled sausages and potatoes with onions in them. They do these things now, but they give them such fancy names, you think, "Oh, that sounds lovely!"

Kathleen Ash

Jug and Bottle, Charlotte Fowler and family

THE VILLAGE SHOP

The village shop was I would say a mile up the country lane. Up this country lane there was a pub one side and the village shop the other side. You could get paraffin at tuppence a gallon. That was for the hurricane lamp. You could buy candles in there. And they sold everything from nails, dresses, food, oil, vegetable, currants, sultanas – all loose from the drawers and they packed them up for you.

The vegetables outside were locally grown. There was a stall outside with two or three big enamel bowls or buckets. One of them had peas in it that had been soaked all night, the other one had butterbeans that had been soaked all night. So if you took your cup or your bowl, it was done by a penn'orth. They were already soaked. Because those hop-pickers needed that to make their soup to go in those billy cans, when they put the old knuckle in and had boiled bacon, that's all they used to have. Because there was no other means of cooking, you see? And from there, that shop, they had everything, absolutely everything. Chicken food, everything, you name it. And it was the post office. You'd buy knitting wool, needles and threads, dresses, wellies. Everything, all in one little tiny shop. It was like Aladdin's cave. The shop keeper was lovely, the old lady was lovely.

And the pillar box was there. And the phone box was there. So if we wanted to make a phone home, which we didn't really because people never had phones – and not many people could use a phone, not then.

The pub was on the corner, and had its own bit of ground that went up round the back. That was the publican's back garden. But twice a week he let one of the bars round the back for the local butcher. And the local butcher used to put his meat in that bar and if we wanted any meat or had missed the butcher on the field, we could go up there and buy a piece from him. He was there twice a week. And then just up the road further still, another mile up – a mile is nothing in those country lanes – there's a farm up there that had all the cows. You could go and buy a pint of skimmed milk for a penny. It was lovely and fresh, but it was only skimmed, rather like water. They'd made the cream out of it. We got what was left. And we were lucky then, because in those days we never had cows' milk, we had tinned milk. The condensed milk. It was only tuppence a tin. That wouldn't go off. In the mornings when we had our breakfast, we never had cornflakes or shredded wheat. We had bread with margarine on it and a bit of condensed milk on it, soaked in a drop of this milk, this skimmed milk. And that was our breakfast. That's what we used to have. But we had a spread of that condensed milk on it first. If we were lucky we used to have a few sultanas on it or a bit of brown sugar. But brown sugar was hardly ever heard of. And if you had bread and jam, you had bread and jam, full stop. Not bread, butter and jam.

Marjorie Balcombe

THE END OF THE DAY

It was a lovely sound, everybody trudging along, their boots all flipping along the road, all really scruffy. It was like people had really toiled, almost, but happily so. You all had to come off at the same time, you couldn't stay, so when he blew the whistle to go, you all went. So everybody was coming down the road and getting to their huts at the same time.

Elaine Jones

When you think of it we must have been exhausted, by the time we came home in the evening. Then we used to have to go and get the wood to light the fire or go shopping. Well, by the time you got washed and had your food, it was time to get the kids into bed. Sometimes the Salvation Army would come down, and you'd all be round the camp fire, having a sing-song. They used to have magic lantern shows on the field, all us kids would be sitting on the ground, with our mums sitting on the chairs at the back. I think the Salvation Army came down to look after the workers. When I look back on it, they gave us pleasure, because we were working all day, and that was the only relaxation we had. They came down on the field too, and they'd get us all singing and you'd have a little talk. You'd have to say your prayers afterwards.

Laura Murphy

When you finished work and went home, children were washed or bathed. The Salvation Army were at Whitbreads, and you could send your children over to them with a penny and a towel and they would bath them. My mother wouldn't let us go in case we caught something off the other children. She was terrible, my mother, so over-protective of us. She put a fine tooth comb through our hair every night. We could play with other children, but she bathed us herself. She got great pots of water and big kettles hanging on hooks over the fire, and of course we always had the old tin bath down there.

Joan Clarkson

Of an evening, the boys would go scrumping. They'd have a keeper patrolling the orchards with a gun. I don't suppose they'd shoot you but that would be enough to frighten you. He'd probably shoot down to the ground. They had a set of dogs with them and their old gun under their arm – on patrol.

When we got home from the fields, we would put the potatoes in the ashes of the fire and that was good for the tea. Always had baked potatoes with margarine in them. There was a man who had a fish shop in Bermondsey. Every weekend he used to come down with his horse and cart and bring all the kippers and haddocks all the way from London, and go to the hop fields and sell them. He'd come down on his horse and cart, start off on Friday night, get down there by Saturday morning, because he'd stop at a pub!

Bill O'Sullivan

Hungry hoppers (photo lent by Elaine Jones)

Photo lent by Whitbread Hop Farm

EVENINGS ROUND THE FIRE

The evenings were terrific. It was lovely getting together round the fire with the piano accordion going. Everyone sang: "My old man said follow the van" ... all the old songs. People used to make up their own words. There was a tiny little pub called the White Hart and we used to sit out there on a little seat, give the children some lemonade, and then come back and cook the dinner. We used to have a really good time.

Florence Burgess

In the evenings, we'd have supper, and then sit around the fire telling ghost stories and frightening the life out of each other. People would tell their life stories too and we'd have a laugh. The people who took a piano put it under what we called the cook-house. We'd have a sing-song and it was lovely. Some of the elders, if they could spare the money, would go over to the pub and have a sing-song or whatever.

Kit O'Connell

We used to have our camp fire and sit round it at night. Skiffle groups were in vogue then. We'd have a tea chest, a broom stick with a rope and a washboard. We didn't have anything like a guitar, but we used to have great fun. "Ghost Riders in the Sky" was one we used to sing, "Yippee-yi-ay", those type of songs. Lonnie Donnegan was a favourite.

My uncle George should have been on the stage really. He could play any instrument he got hold of, and he was a marvellous stand-up comedian, very clever. He had a mouth organ, he could play a piano, if there was one there, anything that came to hand. And my dad used to play a mandolin. We'd sit round the fires with combs and paper, anything that made a noise.

I had quite a good voice when I was young. I used to have my party pieces I used to sing. Ella Fitzgerald was my favourite. It all seems a long while ago. We used to work hard during the day, picking so many baskets of hops, and at night we used to make our own fun.

Ellen Tucker

In the evenings, we used to sit around the fire and tell ghost stories, frighten each other to death. My Auntie Lil was the worst! She used to say that Uncle Shamus had murdered Aunt Victoria round by the standpipe. You see, sometimes the water out of the tap used to be a bit rusty and Auntie Lilian would say, "That's Victoria's blood." She used to tell all the kids that, if you turned the tap on at midnight, blood would run out. This Victoria was just an invention. No one was really murdered, but Auntie Lil was really good at frightening everyone. One night, we were all sitting round the fire and everyone began going off, until I was the last one there. I was just thinking of going to bed when I heard a voice whispering, "Victoria! Victoria!" and I got really frightened. It was Aunt Lil and the others playing a trick on me. I was so frightened I didn't want to move from beside the fire. I found out later they'd planned all that beforehand!

Marie Berry

The Withers family relaxing after a hard day's hopping (photo lent by Elaine Jones, nee Withers)

The mums used to be very happy down there. They'd all come out in the evening time and bring their chairs out round the fire, and sit talking. All us kids were playing out there, we'd be playing ball in the big field. It was very good there. On a wet day, you'd come home and all the wood would be wet and you couldn't get the fire going; it would all be smoking – that would cause a lot of commotion because you couldn't get your dinner, and all the kids would be starving, waiting for a meal 'cos all we'd had was sandwiches all day. By the time the evening came, everybody was really waiting for a good meal. So, if it was wet, you had to go to the cookhouse – it was only like a tin roof. If somebody had sent their kids home earlier, to start the dinner, you'd have to wait for them to cook their dinner before you could use the fire in the cookhouse because there was only room for about three or four fires. If you tried to push in on somebody else's fire – that's when the ructions would start!

Laura Murphy

We used to have concerts. We'd do a concert in the cookhouse every night, if the kids weren't too tired. All the kids would be singing and I used to go and play and sing. Occasionally you'd get someone who'd have a piano accordion. I remember once, somebody had got a piano, and they put it in the cookhouse, and they had a little party. On Saturday nights, you would get them all singing, coming back from "The Bell".

Kathleen Ash

When we'd finished our work, we'd go down the pub and all have a sing-song down there or have a sing-song round the fire but most times, we used to land up in the pub! We used to sit up for hours and hours; nobody wanted to go to bed, because it was so nice: everybody was friendly there.

Ruby Jones

SINGING IN THE DARK

In September it got dark early and there was no point in being outside. We used to have candles and lamps, so you could read. I remember one particular night at Paddock Wood, we were all in the huts, we were lying in bed and it was dark, and we were all singing songs right through the night. Somebody started singing, and I can remember lying there – I did know all the songs at one time – and you just lay in bed and right through the night you'd all sing! It was great. Nothing else to do; it was September, it was dark outside, the fires were finished, and being a child you were in bed that little bit earlier, and you just lay in bed and sang songs.

Lilian Carter

One incident when I went to Paddock Wood was when my brother, Richard, and his wife came for a week's holiday. They had a black spaniel dog called Son. It was very jealous, so when my brother wanted to get into bed at night he used to coax him with chocolate. People were getting fed up with this, and one night a voice piped up "kick it up the arse and let's get some sleep!"

Kit O'Connell

PAYMENT

September 1931

As to what one can earn, the system of payment is this. Two or three times a day the hops are measured, and you are due a certain sum (in our case twopence) for each bushel you have picked. A good vine yields about half a bushel of hops, and a good picker can strip a vine in about ten minutes, so that theoretically one might earn about 30/- by a sixty-hour week. But in practice this is quite impossible. To begin with, the hops vary enormously. On some vines they are as large as small pears, and on others hardly bigger than peas; the bad vines take rather longer to strip than the good ones – they are generally more tangled – and sometimes it needs five or six of them to make a bushel. Then there are all kinds of delays, and the pickers get no compensation for lost time. Sometimes it rains (if it rains hard the hops get too slippery to pick), and one is always kept waiting when changing from field to field, so that an hour or two is wasted every day. And above all there is the question of measurement. Hops are soft things like sponges, and it is quite easy for the measurer to crush a bushel of them into a quart if he chooses. Some days he merely scoops the hops out, but on other days he has orders from the farmer to "take them heavy", and then he crams them tight into the basket, so that instead of getting twenty bushels for a full bin one gets only twelve or fourteen, i.e. a shilling or so less. There was a song about this, which the old East End woman and her grandchildren were always singing:

> *Our lousy hops!*
> *Our lousy hops!*
> *When the measurer he comes round.*
> *Pick 'em up, pick 'em up off the ground!*
> *When he comes to measure*
> *He never knows where to stop;*
> *Ay, ay, get in the bin*
> *And take the fucking lot!*

From the bin the hops are put into ten-bushel pokes which are supposed to weigh a hundredweight and are normally carried by one man. It used to take two men to hoist a full poke when the measurer had been taking them heavy.

With all these difficulties one can't earn 30/- a week or anything near it. It is a curious fact, though, that very few of the pickers were aware how little they really earned, because the price-work system disguises the low rate of payment. The best pickers in our gang were a family of gypsies, five adults and a child, all of whom, of course, had picked hops every year since they could walk. In a little under three weeks these people earned exactly £10 between them – i.e. leaving out the child, about 14/- a week each. Ginger and I earned about 9/- a week each, and I doubt if any individual picker made over 15/- a week. A family working together can make their keep and their fare back to London at these rates, but a single picker can hardly do even that. On some of the farms nearby the tally, instead of being six bushels to the shilling, was eight or nine, at which one would have a hard job to earn 10/- a week.

George Orwell, Collected Essays

On one particular farm, they picked in bushel baskets. So when one was full you knew you'd picked a bushel of hops. When they had the bins in the early days, the measurer would go round and they'd measure all the bins. This particular farm had bushel baskets, so he'd just take the basket away and give out another one. Then he'd have a book to put down what you'd picked. You'd do about forty to sixty baskets a day. You only got eight baskets for a shilling. That's a lot of picking. That was when the hops were very good, the bigger the hops, the less you need to fill your basket. If the hops were bad they were very small. They'd be down to five a shilling. Some years it was worse than others, they could have a bad year for hop growing. Six weeks was a good hopping season, if it'd been a bad year it'd probably only be two weeks. But there'd always be some hops.

Eileen O'Sullivan

Eileen O'Sullivan's father, David Hart, basket picking

Settling up on the last day (photo lent by John Wardley)

STRIKES

There were never arguments over pay. If you were lucky and went to a good farm, you didn't have to go on strike. There were a lot of farms in the area that used to go on strike especially with the travellers. But on our farm the farmer wouldn't allow it – he wouldn't have the travellers.

Kit O'Connell

In the early days, not a lot of people had the money to splash out. I know people that used to go down there and work and after the first week they could go to the office and get a sub out of what they'd earned. They would do that to live. And some of the men wouldn't give the wives any money while they were away. We were lucky; I never had to sub. My husband came down weekends, and gave me my money to live on for the week. Some people went home to bills, rent to be paid. But they didn't care that much, they'd have a holiday, they lived, and finally caught up with some of their debts. We were lucky to be able to keep the money, and either buy the kids new clothes at Christmas or toys. Because it was extra money for us.

One time, at Whitbread's, they called a strike, and we all came out. Nobody really wanted to, but somebody had suggested it, and of course you all had to join in. It didn't last long, only a few days, but we did get an increase in the pay that time. I think we got a little bit more per bushel, perhaps we got a shilling for four bushels instead of a

shilling for five. I think as time went on, hop-picking wasn't regarded as a place to go and earn money. People loved doing it and they still earned, but it wasn't anything like enough money to buy the children's things or something for yourself. There was never any difficulty of getting anybody to go to Whitbread's because it was a real holiday, it was still a holiday. They still went to the fields, they still picked, even when the urgent need for money had gone.

Kathleen Ash

A strike which lasted two days occurred at Castlemain Farm, Horsmonden. Workers went into the hop gardens on Monday morning and left again almost immediately, demanding a reduction in the tally from 5 to $4\frac{1}{2}$.

Work was not resumed until Wednesday morning, and it was announced that the tally would be lowered to $4\frac{1}{2}$.

* * * *

Between 400 and 500 hoppers, mostly Londoners, at Mapelscombe Farm, Farningham ceased work on Wednesday to enforce a demand for four bushels for a 1s., instead of five After a strike lasting three hours the demand was granted and work resumed

SUBS

Every Wednesday or Thursday, you could go to a little office up this long lane at the end of the field, and you could have a loan on what you picked. You only wanted about five shillings, and that would see you through the week. We were all hard up. In Deptford you used to have a day off from school while you had your shoes mended. I never had new shoes. Not until I went to work when I was fourteen. I joined a shoe club then where you paid sixpence a week. You could buy a pair of shoes for a pound. So say there's twenty people, twenty tickets went into that bag and you picked out a ticket. So if you had ticket number eight out of twenty, you waited eight weeks and you got a pair of shoes. And the person that had number nine, she waited nine weeks. Every week one person would get a pair of shoes. And a perm club was the same.

Marjorie Balcombe

We'd be picking at the bins until about Tuesday or Wednesday, and then the money was getting low, so up to the farm and, "How much have I earned?" you'd say. "About £3." "Can I have a rhubarb?" (That was a sub) "How much do you want?" "Can we have £1?". "Yeah, all right then." You'd earned that money, but they used to hate letting you borrow on it!

Bet Easterbrook

We never got rich out of hop-picking. Not one bit. We used to have a loan out of it through the week to buy the food until our menfolk came down. If my mother came home with a five pound note after three weeks work, she'd made a lot of money. And we were all professional pickers because we were brought up on it. But with that five pound she always went and bought something for the home which we couldn't do otherwise. One year, she bought a three piece suite which cost her three pounds, ten shillings. It was rexine, looks like leatherette with a fabric back but quite shiny. That was lovely.

Marjorie Balcombe

PHOTOGRAPHERS

You'd get the photographers come round, and take a picture. Then they'd bring them back and charge you. That was how probably all the pictures come about. Because people wouldn't have had a camera. I don't remember anyone having a camera. They were souvenir photos, but lots of people couldn't afford to buy them anyway.

Elaine Jones

Admiring the "hopping photos" Mrs Neighbour

"THE HOPPING HAT"

When I was about fifteen, I used to be one for dressing up, I was the height of fashion, me. There were these Valencia hats that came out – they were a Spanish style, flat, and you used to wear a rose underneath. People that had money used to buy them. I kept saying to my mum, "I'd love to buy one of these Valencia hats." Well, my mum, she was a widow. She had seven of us kids, all under fourteen years old, so she had a hard life. My mum said to me, "Alright then, when we get down the hop fields, you work hard, and then you can buy one of these hats when we come home." I said, "Oh yes." And I worked like a bloody slave! I stripped me fingers off, and I worked and worked and worked. Mind you, I loved hop-picking, but I had this added incentive for doing it. And I did very well. Anyway, after about three or four weeks, we came home. We went in the kitchen and on the table was this great big paper bag and when we looked inside – there were these great big Valencia hats in it! I went potty! Mrs Gailbrake, one of our neighbours, had got a load cheap for her daughters and she'd bought some for us too! And to think I had worked so hard for one! My mum said, "Never mind love, I'll buy you a new rose." Cost her 6d and 3 farthings!

Minnie Martin

RULES AND CONDITIONS TO BE OBSERVED BY HOP-PICKERS

1. Each bin must be worked by at least two, and not more than three, Adult pickers. Children under 14 may pick, but are in no sense regarded as employed by the Management.

2. Acceptance of a Bin means that the Bin-holder undertakes to work the Bin for the duration of the picking, unless discharged or released by the Management. Bins unoccupied for more than one complete working day will be taken over and the holders' account closed, except in cases where there is evidence to show that reasons for absence were beyond control of persons concerned.

3. Pickers must arrive in the Hop Garden at the time laid down for picking to commence, and will not leave until the last measure of the day has been taken from their Bin.

4. Hops must be picked cleanly, free from bunches and leaves, and all hops must be picked up from the ground around the Bin before moving.

5. Pickers must keep their huts, cookhouses and surrounding area clean, use dustbins provided for refuse, and generally assist in Camp cleanliness. Occupiers of huts are responsible for leaving their huts and area clean and tidy on departure.

6. Firing is put down at each hut every day. Any person helping themselves to firing, or otherwise committing wanton mischief, will be immediately discharged.

7. Dogs are not welcome, and if brought will not be allowed on the farms except on a lead.

8. Anyone trespassing in our own or neighbouring Farmers' Orchards, or Woodlands, or damaging property, will be discharged.

9. All goods brought down by Workers are held by them entirely at their own risk, and the Company does not accept liability for any damage, or loss of effects while on the Farms.

10. Every precaution must be taken against FIRE.

WHITBREAD & COMPANY LTD.,

A LOST PURSE

When we were all going hop-picking, there was a place in Deptford called Robinson's Flour Mills, where they used to grind the flour. It used to come in white hessian sacks, so everybody wanted one of these sacks to make an apron. I had one, all the ladies had one, all the girls, not the men. My mother used to put a big pocket in like the stall holders have, no zip, so that her book – her tally book as she calls it, when they measured out – was always in there and her purse was always in there. Well one day, she was bending over the hop bin, and she lost her purse in the hops. She didn't realise she had lost it until the latter part of the day, so then she sent us round to see Mr Day to say what had happened. "Right," he said, "you come round here with your brothers and we'll find it." And they took us to where the hops are taken in, to the top floor of the oast house and they're spread out on the floor with slats and a fine mesh. It was very hot and the hops were put out to be dried. And it's knee high deep. He took us in there to find that purse. We waded through, we kicked. There were three of us. Like being on the beach with sand really. And we found it.

Marjorie Balcombe

AN UNEXPECTED BANQUET

Once, in 1920, we'd got to the hop fields on the Saturday. My mum had absolutely no money, so we had nothing much to eat. We were hoping for a "sub" on the Monday to buy some food. When Monday came, there was torrential rain, so we couldn't pick, therefore couldn't get a sub. So I went to the orchard, scrumped some apples, then took some swedes and turnips, and took them back to my mum who cooked them for our dinner. Later I went to Horsemonden village and found a 10/- note. I couldn't believe my luck. I went into Walter's stores, bought a loaf, bacon, cheese, corned beef, sugar, butter, tea and some steak. When I got back to the hut, I said to my mum that I fancied some steak for my dinner. She told me not to be so stupid, only in stronger language than that! I then produced all this food, plus the change. I'll never forget her face – she was overwhelmed, burst into tears and kissed the face off me. Her name was Charlotte Wakeling (married name Baldwin) and she was born in Poplar Workhouse in 1878. She'd only ever known poverty and this was like a king's banquet for us. We used to look forward to the weekends when visitors or our dad would come down, and bring us some food

Tom Baldwin

WEEKENDS

My father used to come down to the hop fields to see us every weekend. So, every Friday night we would all be washed up, with our clean jerseys on. We had clip-on ties sewn on our jerseys, so when you put it on you had a shirt and tie all at the same time. Then you were smart, weren't you? We used to get all cleaned on Friday night then we'd be down to the railway station by twelve o'clock Saturday to meet our father, coming down with our sweets from London. We'd wait for the train to come in, and we'd carry his cases up to the hop house hoping to get our sweets. That was the weekly treat for all the boys and girls that used to go down hopping.

Bill O'Sullivan

You took a load of old clothes with you for hop-picking, but when you'd go out at the weekend, you'd dress up! Friday night was Amami night. We'd wash our hair, put the curlers in. Up on Saturday morning and into Maidstone – with your curlers still in – come back with all your shopping and get all washed and changed because the men were all coming down for the weekend ... it was Saturday night! The women would go down the road to the pub with their wellies on and their shoes in their hand. Leave the wellies in the hedge, put their shoes on and go into the pub! Coming back to the farm, you used to put your wellies back on to go down the alley way where the mud was. Coming back of a night-time, my dad would be up the front, in charge 'cos he'd had the light – a big bike torch. Once, he said, "Come on, follow me." and he fell straight down a ditch! I tell you what – I never stopped laughing!

Bet Easterbrook

I used to love weekends, because we used to make a fire at what they called the cook house, and some of the fellows that came down would sit round the fire and play the piano or accordion. We used to have a really good time.

Charlotte Fowler

The men arrive (photo lent by Mike Fitzgerald)

On Saturday, Mum used to do all the washing and there'd be lines and lines all hung out with washing from the whole week, all the kids' clothes. Saturday afternoon was hairwash time, so we all used to have to queue up and have our hair washed, and get in the hut and wash right down in a tin bath. The young ones used to go in first – nice clean bath for the young ones. Well by the time it got to us, all we did was stand in it and ... filthy! But we were washed!

On Sundays, Dad would come down and Mum would get a joint, put it in a baking tin and do all the potatoes round the meat. You'd then take it round to the bakers and the baker would cook it for you for sixpence. You used to write a number on the side of the tin; you'd come back at one o'clock and you'd give them the number and then he would give your joint back again.

Laura Murphy

Billy Hudson takes it easy at Lily Farm, Five Oak Green

Tom Easterbrook and children fishing on the Medway

I used to go fishing on the Medway, take the kids there on the Sunday. We'd make our own rods out of sticks. It was a good holiday.

Tom Easterbrook

At weekends we would go down into Maidstone shopping. Going shopping on Saturday to Maidstone was a real treat. You got pocket money according to how well you had picked hops and a slap-up meal of fish and chips. Mind you, there was only one portion between two of us. On the way back my mum and her friends had a drink in the Railway pub while we had a glass of lemonade and a biscuit.

Sunday roast dinner we used to take to the bakery to be cooked. We would take it at twelve o'clock and call back at two o'clock, on the way home from the pub. Many a time it was mostly eaten before we got back to the huts.

There were often dances in the village. I went to them when I was about seventeen. It wasn't like up in London, of course, but I used to enjoy barn dances and things like that. I would just wear a skirt and a blouse. If you were in London you would get dressed up. I would dance to records with whoever was there. This was normally on a Saturday night, but sometimes during the week as well. We all had a boyfriend down hop-picking. In my courting days I did well with the farmer's son and was hoping to be a farmer's wife. They looked forward to seeing the girls.

The weekends were terrific. Where we were, there was old Granny Brine from Bermondsey. She was a Catholic lady and she used to have an Irish band come down there on her common and that wasn't far from where we were – it was the same farm but another common. They used to play all the Irish songs. They were lovely people, rough and ready but great.

There was a big Catholic community there: Alice Sullivan, Bernie Bowings, Mrs Hicks, Mrs Pilot – I remember them all. Every year we came back and we'd see the same people. Alice Sullivan from Bermondsey is still living, aged eighty-three. She went to Blest's Farm, Mereworth. Well, every Friday she would go back home to see what her boys who were working in the docks were up to. Coming back on the Sunday, she would buy a platform ticket at London Bridge and get to Sevenoaks with it. Then she would go to the ladies' toilet where there always happened to be a window open and she'd get through this, so she never had to pay her fares. She did this for years and if she got caught, she'd bluff her way out.

There used to be some punch-ups on Saturday nights when some of them got too boozed. There were husbands and wives having a punch-up but you never took any notice because if you interfered you used to get hit too. The husbands working in London used to come down for weekends and they'd probably bring a lot of food down from London. Most of the men were dockers. My husband was a docker – he spent thirty-three years in the docks. The men would come down on the Saturday night and go back Sunday evening (or the Monday morning, depending on whether or not they had a hang-over).

Kit O'Connell

Fagin's Den for hard drinking hoppers! (photo lent by Ellen Russell)

The Gannon family at Lily Farm (photo lent by Anne Fitzgerald)

All the week you're done up in an old jumper and a scarf or hat. And your wellies. Everybody had wellies, because you went out and you started picking at seven in the morning when it was still very wet. Then at the weekend you would probably have just everyday things on, but you looked very smart, because all the week you were in jumpers and thick skirts and coats.

Oh you had to boil every drop of water you had, so you usually washed in cold water. The men used to go over and wash at the tap, run the tap and wash, under a cold tap. There was no showers or anything like that. It was a hard life, but it was lovely.

On Sundays the Salvation Army used to come down with their tambourines. It was really lovely, because all the children were washed bright as new pennies, lovely long plaits, and singing and dancing and skipping. The Salvation Army used to come down, but if you were a Roman Catholic you had something different across the fields you see. They used to come down and set it up,

because a lot of them over at Stepney and White Chapel were Roman Catholics. My father was. I'm not. So you chose who you wanted to go to. It was all out in the open. On the common. Oh yes, rain or blow or otherwise, it was there. We used to go and sit on the grass if it was dry. There was no deckchairs, no seats. We used to enjoy it.

On Sundays, the farmer himself and his wife, and his family, used to come out on this wagon, go round the field with all the apples, little tiny apples, throw them out, and we all used to scramble for them. Or you'd hold your apron up and he'd tip the apples in there for you. That was to keep the children and the adults out of the orchards. But I bet everybody where I lived, always had a hopping apple. My father used to go and pick them. He was a rogue, my father, he really was. He used to pick these apples; that one for Mrs Smith, that one for Mrs ... "I must take her back a hopping apple." Everybody had a great big one. Baking apple. You can't eat it, it's too sour.

Marjorie Balcombe

67

WEEKEND VISITORS

The visitors would sleep anywhere, they didn't care! They'd all go to the pub and they'd all have a good gutful of beer. And when they come back from the pub Saturday nights it'd be all pitch black. But you could hear everybody walking along singing away. Once they got outside the huts, it'd be, "Come on, light the fires." They'd have a great big fire, to sit round, with all the beer flowing! Everyone would be singing – lovely! I've heard songs there I've never heard in my life again:

> "When we go down hopping
> Hopping down in Kent
> See old Mother Riley
> Knocking for the rent".

People'd make up the verses as they went along.

Minnie Martin

At Whitbread's, they laid on a festival, and insisted on doing a Shakespeare play. You can imagine – all hop-pickers. Real actors and actresses, they were brought down by Whitbread. I remember this particular night, it was "Twelfth Night". Half of the hop-pickers didn't understand what the actors were talking about. Whitbread's would hold a talent competition, and you'd get the Hop Queen – one of their officials would do the judging. Some of the older women would go in for a laugh. You used to get all that – lots of fun. But then you'd get a nice young girl about sixteen would be chosen. She wasn't necessarily a beauty, but she looked it. She would be our Hop Queen.

Kathleen Ash

All dressed up for the weekend (photo lent by Nell Mason)

"Weekenders" (photo lent by Minnie Martin)

68

THE VILLAGE PUB

Everybody went to the pub at weekends. All your family came at the weekend. All ours came on Sunday, occasionally my father would come Saturday night. Everybody got washed and dressed up, especially the young. The young had a wonderful time, boyfriends and oh, it used to be absolutely marvellous for them because of the freedom. My dad would take us over to the pub and he would buy us a bag of crisps and a lemonade, and then he'd send my sister and me back to the hut, and we would read or play cards.

I was always an avid reader. We learned to read very young. My gran always read. My mother read. My father read. As a family we always read. I joined the library in Bermondsey at the earliest possible age. I think I was about six, and we lived across the road. I used to go to political meetings there with my father because I wouldn't let him move without me. Everywhere he went I had to go with him! Oh yes, I used to go to political meetings. The Red Flag, I grew up listening to that music. The people who lived downstairs were staunch socialists. And during an election that would be a committee room.

Joan Clarkson

In the pubs you were segregated. There was one bar for the homedwellers. Really there were too many hop-pickers to be able to go in a bar, so you sat outside on wooden benches with tables. You had to leave a deposit on your glass. A shilling on a pint glass. But you daren't put your glass down. Once you got your beer and you drank that, then you went back with your glass. If you put it down for a minute, somebody would pinch it and take it back, and they'd get the shilling.

Kathleen Ash

When I was first married, and my kids were little, my husband used to come down hopping with us. He loved it down there, but he didn't like to spend too much time at the bin. He'd pick a few hops, then he'd stop. He'd say, "I've just run out of fags." He'd look at my mum, and he'd give her a wink. Suddenly my mum had remembered something, we hadn't got any paraffin for the lamp or something like that. You see, the pub was just over the road and the two of them would sneak over there.

Minnie Martin

I remember one farm where we got chucked off for singing! We were having a beer one Sunday and we went off to play football. When we come back – the farmer said to come through his main gate, past his house and up to the huts. But we was all singing and made such a noise, we got chucked off the farm! We had to go, there could be no arguing with him.

Tom Easterbrook

On the beer (photo lent by Kathleen Ash)

Now, if you had a couple of bob, you'd go down the pub – you might have to walk about a mile, because you're in the middle of nowhere. The beer was 4d a pint, it was quite good there, because it was strong home brew, you didn't need a lot of it. You'd go to the pub and have a pint and have a chat to different people, from other farms, and then go back around about nine o'clock to sit round the fire. That was your mainstay, the fire going all the time. But by the time you've come home from the pub, and you know you've got to get up at five or six o'clock in the morning, it was time for bed.

The visitors came down at weekends, so it would be back to the pub on the Saturday night! We'd have money now, because we're all working. And it wouldn't take much to get boozy. We'd all come home in a good old mood – don't forget there were no lights down there, so, you have to have torches and you all follow one another back from the pub with the torch, otherwise you get lost in the fields. We kept together on the way back but eventually your eyes get accustomed to it, you know your way by heart. In the meantime, not everybody's gone down the pub, and you can see the fires from the hop huts that'd guide you back. And then you all get around each fire, and you're all telling jokes or talking about different things in general, singing songs, especially if you'd all had a fair old drink, some of the old songs that were going. Sometimes my brother would play the banjo and you'd get other people with a harmonica. So Saturday night was your night. You'd all have a sing-song and that, until around about twelve-ish, and then it would be "Goodnight", because people'd say, "Oi, shut that racket!" Sunday morning, everybody, the visitors included, are washing and getting the fire going again, to boil the hot water. And then the majority of the men would go down to the pub again for another good old booze up. They come back from there, they'd have the Sunday dinner – stew! But you would eat anything, because you was hungry. And then around about four or five, they would say, "Te-da." – they're going home.

Stanley Rose

Opposite the shop was the country pub. When the hop-pickers used to go, all the local people had the saloon bar. You daren't put your foot in that saloon bar. And all the hop-pickers had all the rest of the bar. The hop-pickers coming from Stepney and Wapping were real right rogues – my father was one of them. You bought a glass of beer in that pub, it was 4d a pint.

All the bottom of the glasses were painted black. Why? When you bought a glass of beer, you left 6d or a shilling on that glass. When you took it back, they knew it was theirs because the bottom had been painted black, it hadn't come from nowhere else. And when you took it back, you got your 6d back. And that ensured them that they would take the glasses back, because 6d was a lot of money then.

But, my dad as I said, was a rogue. He trained us, much to my dismay now, to make money for him. Say an old man just bought a pint, then he put it down, went out to the loo, left his pint on the table there. When he come back it was gone. Because we nicked it! And we took it back to get the shilling back. Everybody's glass looked the same, so how could he prove it was his glass? We made the money for our dad. And we always got a packet of sweets or something.

Everybody came at weekends, the men came down for the weekend. They'd come down and see their wife and mum. And it was lovely. And you wouldn't think the women were the same people at weekends that you saw in the field in the week. All in their Sunday best and shoes – because we had wellies all the week. But you see, they got the beer and then they all got jolly. It was all "Knees up Mother Brown," and "Take me back to dear old Blighty," and all the old cockney songs. The pearly kings and queens used to come down with them for the weekend as well. And it was real right knees up. It was lovely. But all those local people stayed in that little bar out of the way because if they come out, there was lots of punch ups! They were all the worse for drink when they came down weekends. Lots of punch ups there! So the locals just sat in there out of the way.

The little village shop had a great big plant outside called pampas grass. Being children, we'd never seen this, and we didn't know what it was. In September, it's just coming out in white stalks. So if you slit that stalk, you've got a lovely silvery bloom underneath, haven't you? Well, my dad used to jump this fence at the shop, and he used to strip those flowers while everybody was having a punch up across the road by the pub! This pampas grass is decorative, and all the flowers are enormous, and they've got rough leaves. If you don't watch you'd scratch your skin. He cut these things off, and they're just one stalk. And once you peel that outside cover off you've got your bloom. You can peel it off. It's not nature's way, but that was my dad's way. And it used to make a lovely vase of flowers for us at home. And all the neighbours. And Mrs Smith. "I'll get you one."

Anyway, the police got to hear there was somebody in this lady's garden taking these plants. And he come up to us, and he said, "The police are about," he said. "They're after me for taking these things." He said, "I've got some. But, I'll show you where I'm going to put them." He stood them up and he put them down his legs. The police came up and said, "We're looking for a man that's cutting all those things down." He said, "Not me officer, I couldn't even bend, I've got two bad legs." Us children looked at him and thought, "Oh, God, and there we are, going to church and all that, and he goes to church as a Roman Catholic." I thought, "May God forgive you." He never hurt anybody, but it was all for the sake of the family, if you know what I mean. He had a great sense of humour. It was hilarious. I wouldn't have missed it for all the tea in China. Happiest days of my life.

Marjorie Balcombe

My father used to come down to the farm at weekends and all these farms used to have a little pub down the road. He and his father-in-law would never leave a pub until it was time – they'd be the last ones out. The way back from the pub was across the green, where there was a big oak tree. By this tree there was this pond with all green leaves on top – very good camouflage. You go round the tree and you're all right. But my father wanted to take the short cut and went straight into the pond. He was a very big man, my father, and his father-in-law was a very, very small man. Well, father-in-law had to try and pull him out. The harder he tried to pull him out, the further he was going in. Anyway, it got worse and worse. In the end, the gypsies came and got them both out – 'cos they'd both gone in by this time! When they got back, my mother was up in arms! You see, my father lost a leg in the First World War, so he had an artificial leg. And there they were ... it was Saturday night, they'd been down the pub and his leg was in a right state – wet through! The rooms we had were small with rafters across the top. Well, he had to hang his leg, his false leg, over the rafters to dry out!

Bob Bennett

Something that always fascinated me was that you'd go down there on a Sunday, people in their early 20's, and they'd all come down, dolled up and suited up. See the photos of them. My dad going down in a suit! Can you imagine these days going down in a suit on a boiling hot Sunday?

(Photo lent by Tom Easterbrook)

Bob Bennett's father and grandfather – before *the soaking!*

Weekend drinking! (Ellen Russell's family)

We used to go to the pub Saturday night. We used to take the kids down with us because you didn't know whether to leave them or not, so we'd take them down with us.

My brother-in-law had an old Maria and he used to drive the whole family down to the pub in that. We couldn't get in the pub. It was too full, so we bought a couple of new white buckets – you know the white enamel buckets we used to use for water. We took them in the pub and filled them up! You had to pay a shilling deposit on the glass. In the end we got our own glasses so we never wanted theirs.

And you might not believe this, but we had an organ, a little organ – you know these little church organs, we had one of them. It belonged to us, my husband and me. Well we took it down with us. And we got the organ at the back of the van at the pub and we got my brother sitting up there playing it. Everybody dipping their glasses in the beer buckets, and oh, it was fun! As they emptied the buckets out, so they all clubbed in and filled them up again.

The locals didn't like it. You got the old pub dances: "Knees up Mother Brown", the "Conga" and all that lark. And you'd get a long line of us, with a little kid in here, and then you'd get a great big man up front. It was really fascinating.

We'd sing "Nellie Dean", "Bill Bailey", "Drunk last night, and drunk the night before", "Mother Kelly's Doorstep", because I've got a sister-in-law named Kelly! Ooh yes, you'd always got someone to give a song. I'd do it myself many a time. Me and my husband used to do a duet, all fancy stuff. "Rose of Tralee". He used to sing that

beautiful. They used to get him to sing, "Rose of Tralee", "Danny Boy", and all that.

Sunday afternoon, my nephew used to play the organ on the common for the service for the kids. We'd sing hymns: "All Things Bright and Beautiful", "We Plough the Fields and Scatter".

Ellen Russell

Us men would get our beer money Sunday morning and we'd wait for opening time at the "Hop Pole". My brother'd watch the pub door to see when it would open. "We'll be first", he said. But outside the pub, there was a little grass island and as the pub door went "click", five heads come out the grass! All these fellows were hiding in the grass waiting for the pub to open! The barman at The Yarrow never worried about the hop-pickers. He'd say "Time, please!" and if no-one had heard him, he'd get his copper's helmet out and put it on – he was the local bobby as well!

Tom Easterbrook

I remember the Saturday nights in the pub when I was a child. Some of the women had beautiful voices. They had all their old hopping songs. Traditional songs they used to sing. Bermondsey was an Irish area, so when our lot got down the pubs in Kent, there'd be singing! Somebody would just start off a song by themselves ... "I'll Take You Home Again, Kathleen" ... then somebody else'd do "Danny Boy". Sometimes, someone would play a mouth organ. The hopper's bar was bare of furniture. They used to take the pictures off the walls – they didn't trust us!

Bill O'Sullivan

72

Menfolk from the Fitzgerald clan at the Railway Bell, Tonbridge

A LANDOWNING HOPPER

My grandad was well known down at Bank Farm, and one day he goes to see the governor, Mr Thomas. "Good morning," he said, "I've got all the hoppers here together." "Good morning Michael," the farmer said, "Everything alright?" "Yes. By the way sir," he said, "Can I have a sub?" He said, "You don't have subs. You're not picking the hops." "This is a special case." he said. "They've come all the way from London, they've not got a bit of bread or nothing to eat. They're all starving." So the farmer said, "Well, I'll go in the house and see what's in there." So he goes in and comes back with about thirty bob. "That's how much; thirty shillings." "Thank you very much sir, thank you." So he goes to the women and gives them about half a crown each. The rest of it, him and about ten of the blokes they go up to the pub.

The man who used to have the pub was a city gent, Harry Weller. They'd walk in the pub, the blokes, about six blokes. "Good morning Harry." "Oh, good morning, Alright?" "Yes." "What would you like?" "Six nice pots of bitter." "That'll be £1." "You'll have to put that to my account", my grandfather said. "Your account? You never paid me the last time you were here!", he said, "What about that?" "I know, I know, quite right," said my grandfather, "but think of the double payment you'll get this time."

He was one of the best characters you could ever meet. A successful man in that he done everything he wanted to do in life. Done exactly what he wanted to do. Completely selfish. He bought a bit of land down there, he'd go down there and sleep and drink, and do exactly what he wanted.

Lived there most of the time like a recluse, him and his wife, she was as bad. They'd rough it down there.

She was a lovely woman, his wife, very nice woman. But characters, weren't they? To look at him you'd think he was an old tramp. But he'd buy the land, he'd go to all the auctions. Very shrewd man. His bit of land down there was worth a lot of money, it had building permission.

He had an old bike, you'd see him riding round and round. Stopped at a pub one day at Matfield, had a pint, sitting there and a bloke come up to him and says, "Hello Mike, come up to buy the wood?" He said, "What wood's that?" "Over there." he said, "It's for sale." "When's it going to be sold?" "In the back of the bar here." "Oh yes? I'll have a look in at that," he said. He goes in there, about a dozen people in there to buy the bit of wood. They're all bidding up but he hasn't even seen the wood yet, and don't know where it was even. They've bid up, bid up. "Right, what's your name?" "Mr Fisher." he said. His name's Fitzgerald, actually, but he says Fisher. "Right, that'll be so and so and so and so." "I ain't got no money on me sir." "What do you mean, got no money; just bought a bit of land, got no money?" "I'll get it tomorrow, my wife's got it." So they let him have the land, sold to him. Went down the next day with her. They paid for it. A forest it was. He had a whole lot of land near the Medway.

He sold some of it. The bloke who had the farm next door used to let his sheep come through and eat all the grass. So he said what's he bought it for, he paid good money for that? Eventually he got fed up with it and he sold it for about five times what he paid for it.

Mike Fitzgerald

The pub near our farm was called the White Hart. They used to just have one bar for the hop-pickers and they would take all the furniture out of the room! All you'd have in it was the wooden table and the wooden bench all the way round. I suppose the pickers would have a fight or something, or over would go the beer. They wouldn't appreciate furniture. And I suppose they could get more people in. Some pubs used to charge 6d or a shilling on the glass. So you used to keep your glass all night long. So if you went in the pub and you wanted a drink, you'd have your pint of beer in a pint glass, they used to charge you a shilling extra, so when you took the glass back empty, they'd give you a shilling. If you lost your glass, you lost your shilling.

Bill O'Sullivan

At the weekend everybody had a strip wash in their hut with a bit of hot water if they were lucky, and everybody would come out really looking nice. But on the pub doors it always said, "No hop-pickers or gypsies in this bar." So you always had to go round. It was accepted, although some local people used to like to mix with the hop-pickers because it was a bit more fun. There'd be lots of singing and dancing. During the year I don't suppose there was about ten people in the pub. All of a sudden during the hop-picking season the landlord must have made a fortune. Especially at weekends with all these men coming down from London and just singing and dancing and goodness knows what in the pub.

You'd all have to see your way home with the torch because the lanes were so dark – I can't imagine anything being as dark as it used to be – so you'd have to have a torch and you'd go along, and find out where you had to be.

My grandad seemed to be around most of the time. But he'd leave the bin about half past ten and when we came back at four o'clock, he'd be asleep outside the pub, snoring away. Drunk. He'd just look at his clock, half past ten, off he'd go and that would be it. He used to walk away with his boots tied round his neck by the laces. He'd wear shoes, but he'd always have his boots with him, in case he needed them for working! Gran used to say, "Go and get him from that pub! His dinner's here." Or she'd take it up there. Take it up to the pub and just give it to him. Over his head I think sometimes. He'd shout, "Go away, woman!" He wasn't interested in eating anyway, he just wanted to have a drink. But he loved it down there.

Elaine Jones

FLIES ON THE WALL

There was a pub near the station at Paddock Wood, and we used to go up there of a night-time. I was used to living in London, and you weren't allowed in pubs there. I've stayed outside so many pubs because Dad drank twice a day, and I used to play outside. When I went to Paddock Wood we were actually allowed in the pub, providing we were tucked up in a corner somewhere. We heard all the songs and performances and the goings-on that the grown-ups did. We were ushered in and told to sit down and behave ourselves. Well you did, because you knew that you weren't allowed in pubs. It was an adult area.

Lilian Carter

"Our crowd" (photo lent by Bet Easterbrook)

FRIENDSHIPS AND FEUDS

There was a lot of gypsies down there hop-picking. They kept in a crowd on their own, but they joined in the merriment in the pub in the evening. Some of them might have a fiddle and accordion and we would have music and a bit of dancing.

Bill Webb

It didn't matter if you were from Liverpool or Birmingham, the homedwellers called you "Londoners", "Bloody foreigners, coming down here taking our jobs!" But they couldn't manage it on their own, there were only about thirty people living in the village.

Tom Easterbrook

I used to put some of the Londoners up in my own house. They'd sleep on the floor and everything! First of all I started with just a couple of them. I said, "Oh, save you going in the hop huts." Because they used to have straw mattreses in the huts, you know, straw pillows and that. We had a big copper in the kitchen to boil the water in. My husband would get the cold water from the well and I'd fill the copper. We used to have a long tin bath by the fire, and all of our Londoners used to take turns to have a bath in that. We had to keep filling the copper and emptying this great tin bath, but it was great fun really!

Saturday night they used to go to the pub – as you know, Londoners do like a little drink. Of course, Londoners are dead scared of the dark. They really are. When they used to go to the pub – my husband was terrible! He used to get behind a hedge and shake it and make the Londoners run and scream!

We looked forward to the Londoners coming down. It was all the Londoners from the East End, Walworth way, that picked on our farm and most of their names were Ward. They'd write and tell me that they'd be coming down, they'd be so pleased. My children learned to call the mum Nanny Ward. Her sons and daughters used to come down with her and her husband would visit at the weekend. My place was choc-a-bloc! After the war I used to go up now and again to see them where they lived in Lorrimore Road. To us, it was our holiday too, because we never saw anybody else all year round. They never came down hop-picking to earn money; they came for a holiday. And they really had to work hard because they had to pick thirteen bushels for a shilling. Of course the kids would go scrumping – that's only natural! The boss used to tell them off about it, and they used to run!

Alice Heskitt

The homedwellers resented us. Well, they always used to call us "the dirty Londoners". They didn't pick with us and they didn't come in the huts at all. If you went round the town shopping it would be: "Oh, it's those London kids again!" If you go in the bakers, "Oh, two of them London kids; get them out the shop!" ... because we were brazen, weren't we?! I mean, we were the London kids! I can't say they disliked us – they weren't really happy towards us. Perhaps because we were wild. Mum only had two boys; most of us were girls. Some of the boys were a bit wild *and* some of the dads when they would come down at weekends and maybe have a little tipple too much!

Laura Murphy

My family got friendly with the people down on the farm and instead of having a hut, one of the homedwellers, Mrs Smith said, "Well I've got rooms here you can have." So we used to stop there. We were happy there – it was like a home from home. The only thing I didn't like was Friday night, bath night and liquorice powder. That was your medicine. I spat it out every time. I hated it. Even when we were hopping we were clean. Every night we had our good wash down and old Mrs Smith gave us a bath on Friday nights.

We had a man called Mr Manners, who had a car and he used to take us down to the hop fields. There would be four of us, Mum, me and my sister and Dad. Hop-picking was in our family, from Grandma, Grandad and right back. It was a tradition. I liked the atmosphere; the meat man coming round, the lollypop man coming round, the baker coming round the fields. And in the evenings, you'd sit round the fire cooking. If Mum wanted shopping done in town, that was my job in the morning, to walk up town with the other half a dozen kids that were sent on errands. We'd go up to the little shop that used to serve us with cheese and bacon. On Friday night the fish and chip man came round the huts.

Doris West

Homedwellers didn't mix very well: they didn't like the London people. They would pick on the farms but they would pick in their own little section. They didn't go in where the Londoners were. We'd see them going down of a morning, and I remember my mother saying, "Hurry up, the homedwellers are going!" You'd see them all going along with their prams. They were pretty poor. They used to have these prams like basinets and they'd go down to the fields about half past six when it was just getting light. They'd always be first in the hop fields. The homedwellers used to grab all the big hops, so that when you went down it was all the little ones. The farm managers also were local people, so they'd look after their own people and put them where the best hops were. They didn't want to really mix in with the Londoners. We were pretty rough people compared with their way of life. Really rough in our old boots and pullovers! They probably didn't see anybody in those days from one year to another so when the Londoners came down it was like people coming from another planet. We had boisterous ways!

Eileen O'Sullivan

1962 The Bowers' family outside their hut

TRAVELLING FOLK

There used to be a family of gypsies would come down to the hop fields. They looked just like the pictures you see, they would sit and smoke their clay pipes for hours on end. They never caused any trouble, the Romanies, the proper Romanies.

Charlotte Fowler

Some of the pubs wouldn't have gypsies. They'd have a big notice up. "No Travellers served here." So they weren't allowed to go. Where we were hop-picking, the farmer wouldn't have them on the farm. Gypsies mainly picked fruit, which was out at the same time as the hops. The gypsies used to put all their decorated caravans inside the farm – right in the middle of where the orchards were. They'd stay there until they'd completely picked all that orchard, then they would move on to another one. They used to move all round the Kent area like that, picking.

The dockers from Bermondsey were a tough lot of people and the gypsies were too, so you had the two lots. "We're better than you lot." Sometimes, after a few pints, there'd be an argument and then that would start things off. You'd get a few men who'd had one too many pick up someone's glass and say, "That's mine!" Then there'd be fisticuffs. But after the years of going there, you got used to all these kinds of people.

When we picked at Bodiam, women used to come hop-picking from Hastings. Their husbands were fishermen, where they didn't earn a lot of money. On one side of the common, we used to have Hastings people, and on the other, all the London people. But they all mixed in together.

Bill O'Sullivan

There was a lot of gypsies around. They'd be friendly, but there was a bit of hostility there too, between the gypsies and the pickers. The old distrust that people have of anybody different, I think, that's all there was. I don't remember a lot of hostilities, but I heard there was. They didn't mix; they didn't want to mix, the gypsies and didicots, they seemed to want to be separate. But that abated, I'd say, as the years went on. Later on the younger didicots and gypsies did, because I remember one that was always round our hut, chatting and talking.

Elaine Jones

My cousin used to suffer with warts on her fingers. One year she came down hopping with us, and this old gypsy took my mum to the side and she showed her a plant to put on her warts. She broke it up and as the sap ran out, she rubbed it all over my cousin's hands. The old gypsy said to my mum, "Do that for seven days, and they'll go." She was right, they did go and they never came back! I never could find that ruddy plant again!

Vi Lewis

HOPPING ROMANCES

He was very nice. I can remember his name, Willy Bean. He used to live down there. On Sunday afternoon he took me walking, we went off round the country lanes. When we come back to London, that was the end of it.

Laura Murphy

You got your money at the end of the season. But you could go and have a sub. You could go to the office and sub some of your money. The office was just a little hut with a stable door and a little bench. You asked them to give you so much of your money in advance, and then at the end of the season when you'd finished you got your whole amount. One of the farm workers, the foreman, would deal with that. You didn't get much contact with the people who owned the farm. More contact with the farm boys. We had this tall one, Cyril, with a very strong Kentish accent. He used to drive the drays. All the little girls idolised him. He used to have a laugh and a joke, and humour them. As little girls we used to see this great big tall man, with lovely curly hair, and we all liked him. I wished he'd ask me for a date. I was only about fourteen. One of the girls was quite glamorous, and he took her out to the pictures. They used to write to each other, and keep in contact, but she didn't marry him. I don't know who he married.

Flo Batley

I had a romance at fruit-picking. She lost the meat and I found it. One day they went to have their dinner, have a break while they were picking gooseberries. They sat over the hedge and I sat there. All of a sudden, such a commotion: "What's that? Someone's got my meat!" I said, "Is this yours?" "Yes, that's mine, greedy sod!" And that was our first meeting.

Mike Fitzgerald

Occasionally, you'd get a couple that would just meet each year and in between times they might meet up somewhere in London, just for a day, it was never more than that. They used to call them, "a hopping chap"; "She's got a hopping chap." Maybe someone would have a romance with one of the farm labourers. Not actually the farmer's son. Bit too up market! Everybody more or less kept a close watch on everybody else. Sometimes, if one woman was a bit too friendly with the measurer they'd say, "Oh look at her. She's only doing that for what she can get out of him." See if she can get an extra measure you know!

Eileen O'Sullivan

There was the farmer's son down on the hop fields and he fell for my sister Violet. He loved her. He was always talking about them getting married and settling down there. But she certainly wasn't the country type! She used to laugh at him and say, "Cor blimey, Country Bumpkin! You want me to be a Mrs Country, well I'm not doing it!" He came up to London one weekend after the hop-picking was finished and he brought a great big bag of vegetables, everything! "Oh!" I said, "He's a lovely fellow. Encourage him!" My mum said, "Yes, ask him to come again!" But Violet wouldn't have him.

Charlotte Fowler

Charlotte Fowler and her parents by the huts

A helping hand (photo lent by Minnie Martin)

I had a "Hopping Sweetheart" called Johnny Warren. I thought he was handsome this Johnny Warren. Once a year I'd see him down hopping because he was a home-dweller. We never ever spoke, I just used to see him go by. And every year we went down hopping, me and Sheila used to go to the white gate, just to catch sight of Johnny and his friend Ronnie. We'd wait for hours and hours to see them. They'd walk by and we'd go, "Hello," and they'd go "Hello," and that was it! Every year this went on. So one year he got a bit brave, did Johnny. I don't know how he asked me, but we ended up going to the pictures, me and Johnny and Sheila, my friend. Sheila was ever so noisy – like a mouse! We met him at the bus stop, got on the bus. He never spoke one word. Went in the pictures, saw the film, had our Horlicks when we came out, in the coffee bar and got back on the bus. He never spoke a word. He got off the bus at his stop and never even said goodnight!

That night was the first night of ITV. Sheila and I got off the bus and started to walk back to the hop huts. You know what trees look like when you're walking through the dark – terrifying! I thought they looked like people! We'd never been on our own in the dark like that. Walking along, looking at those trees, and they were like gnarled faces. And we were walking faster and faster and faster. All of a sudden, it started to thunder and lightning. Well, my Nanny used to hide under the table when it thundered, she used to hate thunder, it would put the fear of God into her. She'd taught me to do the same. So the rain is just coming down and I thought we were going to get struck by lightning.

So we knocked on a homedweller's door – we didn't have a lot to do with the homedwellers but we knocked there, terrified. A woman came out, she said, "Oh come in. Come in and get changed." She took our shoes and dried our feet. She said, "It's ITV tonight!" We didn't have a telly at home – we didn't know what she was going on about. "ITV tonight." she said. Anyway, we were there until about 11 o'clock, because the husband didn't want to miss any of this new channel. We watched the telly and it was still pouring with rain and lightning outside.

In the end she said, "You'd better get the girls home now." So he got this big tarpaulin cape thing out and we sheltered underneath it. This homedweller was quiet, didn't say much. So we walked along with him back to the huts. None of us spoke. He saw us to the gate. "Go on now, off you go." That's all he said to us. It seemed then that there was a big gap between the Londoners and the homedwellers – they were completely different to us. Sheila and me didn't know what to say to the poor man.

Anyway, we got home and Sheila said, "I'm just going up to the cookhouse to have a fag." So she got a light out of the fire and lit this fag. Then we heard shouting and hollering. It was my uncle Ted. He never swears usually but this night, he got hold of me, murdered me. "Wait until your father comes down here, I'll tell him what you are. I know what you're getting up to." He's bashed the daylight out of poor Sheila. They'd had search parties out and all the farm was out looking for us!

Anne Fitzgerald

The huts at Whitbread's were in blocks of four. There was one lady in one hut and another lady next door, both were stone deaf, absolutely stone deaf. So you can imagine, we used to get the shouting and hollering sometimes! The one in that one, Aunt Jenny, used to be a real laugh. She used to be up sometimes at three o'clock in the morning, because she did not have a clue what the time was, bang on the wall for Mrs Roberts, who was also stone deaf and she'd be shouting, "Eh? What?" "It's time to get up." "Eh?" Two lovely old people. Aunt Pol had a Downes Syndrome daughter called Joyce who loved to be with my children. She would rock the pram and she would walk it up and down. When Aunt Pol's husband used to come down every weekend, they used to like to go and have a drink. So Joyce used to stay with me. Aunt Pol knew I would look after her.

Kathleen Ash

Lola Berry with her mother, Ria, and her sisters Joyce and baby Maria

A HOPPING THIEF!

Once, in about 1948, we got a message going around the camp that the farmer was checking up as he had had so many apples stolen. Every family rushed around hiding their stocks. My aunt Lizzie, mum's sister, had her pram there and it had a false bottom (all prams were made like this). She hid her apples in there and put the rest in a multi-coloured knitted shawl and hid them in the woods at the end of the huts.

The farmer checked every hut and must have thought that we were the most honest hoppers he'd ever had. When he had left, auntie Lizzie went to get the shawl, it had gone!

Some thieving so-and-so had stolen it. Everyone was up in arms that someone could steal from one of our own. A few days later, someone returned the shawl minus the apples. It was so colourful that everyone knew it was my aunt's. We never did find out who had the apples.

Jean Simmer

GROWING UP

My first year of staying home and *not* going hopping was when I was sixteen. In those days, you got murdered if you came home late and I came in late, so I got grounded. But then my dad said, "Hop it," and he sent me down to my mum. He took me to London Bridge Station, threw me in the train and said to the porter, "Don't let her off until Tonbridge!" So I was down hopping after all! Two of my friends down there were going out and I asked to go with them. We went over to Hoppers, where we'd go dancing. When we came out, there were some fellows there who said, "Do you want a lift?" We said, "Yes." Anyway, they've took us the wrong way, it was going to take us hours to get home and I'd been grounded! Anyway, when I *did* get in, my mother really did start on me – she threw a cup of tea at me but I ducked and it went all over her curtains. My nan came flying in and jumped on her back. It was all over being about twenty minutes late! But when you think about it, it was worrying for them. I'd already been grounded!

Lola Berry

Lola and Joyce Berry

HEALTH AND SANITATION

The gypsies used to use the hops for medicine as a herbal cure. When the gypsy families were down there, nobody was ill. If the kiddies started to get a bit croupy, they'd cut an onion up and put brown sugar on it, leave it overnight, drain it off the next morning, "Here y'are girl, give her a teaspoonful of that, three times a day." My husband had a gnat bite, and it went poisoned. The old gypsy came up and she said, "Got any Sunlight Soap? Give us a bit of that, girl!" She got a bit of clean rag, scraped the soap on it with a bit of sugar, put it on his arm. The next morning, he had a big hole where it had drawn it out, drawn all the poison out.

Bet Easterbrook

When I was a kid, I weighed about two stone and I was deadly white – but there was nothing wrong with me. My Mum always had me up the doctors, "Tom's not well, shall I take him down the country? I think he needs a holiday, doctor." You see you needed a certificate to get off school, if she got one for me, then the whole family could go ... so I was the hopping excuse!

Tom Easterbrook

Hops were wonderful for earache or toothache – it must be the dried hops – not just what you pick. And if you make a pillow and put them in the oven to get hot, and a child's got earache or toothache, bring it out and put it on the sore place, they would soon go to sleep. Because of the smell. Wonderful it is for toothache or earache or if you can't sleep.

Alice Heskitt

We all used to get belly aches because we all used to have to share the one toilet out the back. I think they used to come round and put lime down it, and it was supposed to have been kept clean, but with the children and the fruit we were eating I don't think it was very ... well ... very nice to talk about!

Laura Murphy

There was a girl that used to come down who was an invalid. I never knew what was wrong with her but she'd be carried about in a long wicker basket, like a stretcher. She'd be laid amongst the hops while we were picking because people believed that breathing in the sulphur from the hops made you well. I know it was good for asthma and chest complaints.

Doris West

I was ill, I was very anaemic and had to be put on Parrish's food to build me up. My mother thought she would get me away if she could. So she wrote to my aunt and she said yes she'd have me. So we went down there and the smell of the hops and being in the country really did me good.

Mabel Wilson

Kent Messenger, 1933.

One of my brothers once got really drunk and he fell into the cess pool. No one would touch him. The toilets were in a tin shed which just had a bar across, but they were always putting lime down there so it wasn't overpoweringly horrible. We used to go up to the woods because you can't be too careful.

The farmer we went to had hot water, so we were quite lucky. He had a big boiler up near the sheds, but you could only have hot water at certain times. We used it for washing up and Friday night was bath night. We used to take a big tin bath and we would wash in our own hop hut, one at a time. You would shut the hut door and lie there.

Kit O'Connell

"Pickers get more orderly every year," said a publican.

Kent Messenger September 1933

A British Red Cross Society's dispensary

The toilets were just a box like a watchman's hut, and you went in there, shut the door and there was a board across, and you just sat on the board with a big hole underneath it, and disinfectant in it. There were two or three toilet huts and people used to line up and use it all day long. They used to come and put stuff down it afterwards. Then they'd go and dig a hole farther away, shift it over there. They'd probably put a fruit tree in there afterwards!

Harry Demarne

The toilets must have been five hundred yards way from the huts. One for the men and one for the ladies. They were vile. It was just a galvanised tin hut with a wooden door and a bolt. It was a hole in the ground. That was the hole in the ground and just the piece of wood across there with like a half a seat on it, and if you didn't hold it tight mate you'd gone down that hole! They were all wise to it and didn't fall down, but it was vile. They did used to go round and put stuff down it, but eventually that hole was closed up and the hut was moved someplace else. But it was always well across the field.

Marjorie Balcombe

We had two toilets and they were like square boxes with a round hole, and they put lime down them every week, but I don't think anybody used them. You used to see people walking off the farm and they'd be going to find a field somewhere.

Elaine Jones

A DANGEROUS CORNER!

The toilet facilities were horrible. There was a wooden cubicle right across a muddy field. It was just a hole with a plank across, which had a hole in it. The smell was revolting. Everyone used to avoid it as much as they could. If we only wanted to wee, we would hide in the woods and do it.

Mary Baldwin

I was walking through the tunnels (the hops grew tall and towards each other, creating long tunnels) and as I turned a corner, I saw two women squatting down, with their underclothes down. I retreated instantly and stood perfectly still, pushing myself into the hops, with my eyes tightly shut, in case they saw me and thought I was a Peeping Tom.

A rumour went round that one of the farm hands used to feed the pigs on the toilet slops and he became known as "Old Dirty 'Orrible".

Tom Baldwin

The creche at Whitbread's Hop Farm

THE HOSPITAL SHED

If we wanted a doctor, there was the shed about a half a mile up the road, run by the Red Cross. They used to come down there certain times of the day, every day, including Saturday and Sunday, and if you wasn't well, you had to go to that shed. They called it the hosptial shed, and you gave them what you could. If you'd got a sore throat or a bad head or eyes, that was our doctor there. They never give you a prescription. Any ointment or tablets or whatever, they gave it to you while you were there. They watched you take it. "Come back tomorrow and we'll give you another lot." They didn't trust you. I wasn't well and they gave me some stuff in a glass. I'll never forget it as long as I live. It was vile. I said I didn't want it, and they held my nose and held me down. It was so vile I bit this glass so hard I broke it! My brother says, "Do you remember when you bit that glass and broke it?" And I had to go back every day.

Marjorie Balcombe

Among the many people working hard and doing an immense amount of good are the doctors, nurses and V.A.D.'s attached to the British Red Cross Society's dispensaries and camps. These are at Tudeley, Hunton, Yalding and East Farleigh. All the ailments of the hop-pickers are attended to free of charge.

* * * *

Miss Chenevix Trench, the Hon. County Secretary, is in charge of all the camps, and makes her headquarters at the Tudeley Camp. Here there is one dispensary run by a nurse and seven V.A.D.'s.

* * * *

So far at Tudeley, several cases of burns and cuts have been dealt with, while the removal of a child suffering from scarlet fever has been carried out.

* * * *

On Wednesday evening Tonbridge Fire Brigade was called to Badsell Farm, Five Oak Green, where a hoppers' hut was burnt to the ground, and an adjoining one was damaged.

Kent Messenger September 1933

RED CROSS HUT

We used to have a Red Cross hut just alongside the common – which was full every night with kids being there with their stings and bites! But it was smashing because you'd get a dolly bandage – which nobody had ever seen before. You know one of those bandages on your finger, which the Red Cross do properly, so it's all like a finger stalk. Oh we were so proud of all that. That was the thing if you cut your finger!

Elaine Jones

THE HOPPERS' HOSPITAL

I've always worn make-up, lipstick, powder, everyday I'd put it on – even hop-picking. One year, I went to the hop fields, determined to get a tan. I had lovely hair when I was young, a real mop, and this year I'd had my hair permed. I didn't wear any make up because I was going to get myself a lovely tan. And suddenly my lips startd to swell up – big blisters all round my lips. I was in agony with the stinging. It was terrible. I looked like a bleeding monster!

There was a little Hoppers' Hospital, all the people used to go there with bee stings, things like that. I went to the hospital and saw the doctor. He said to me, "Oh dear. This is not a bite. You're so dry. Do you ever use any cream on your face?" So I said, "Yes I do, I've always used make-up. But I'm not using lipstick because I want to get a nice tan." He said, "Well, I suggest that you go back to using lipstick, because you're so used to this oil on your skin. Directly you get back, put some stick on." I went back and I put lipstick on my lips, on top of the blisters, you can imagine what I looked like! Then I couldn't stop scratching my hair, my beautiful permed hair! I thought I really was licey. But the sun was so hot down there, I couldn't stop scratching. My mum said, "That'll stop you putting all that muck on your face. You want to be like me, drink all the green water you can." Every time she boiled cabbage, she'd keep a cup of the green water, put pepper and salt in it and drink it. She'd say, "Never mind about you laughing at me and my green water: do you ever see any pimples on my face? Ever see any scabs on my face? No, because I drink the green water!"

Minnie Martin

LOCAL TENSIONS

Someone was very, very ill, and we went to the local doctor and he wouldn't come with us. About twenty of us went back to get him, but he refused to come back to the huts with us and threatened to call the police. Well, we all shouted out at him, and he fetched the police to break up our demonstration. The police just moved us on. We were always brought up to believe the police were right, so we just obeyed them.

Hop-pickers' Medical Mission Hut, Horsmonden

That woman died afterwards. They took her away to the hospital and she just died. It was a thing that could happen, but he should have seen her. I think local people resented the hop-pickers because they came back from the pub singing at the top of their voices. I suppose they were in a quiet village and they hadn't had that sort of thing. Every September when the hops were ready, the Londoners came down, showed off a bit and got up the backs of the locals. Of course the shopkeepers and the publicans loved it because they'd do a wonderful trade.

Harry Demarne

A HEALTHY LIFE?

You had a little wooden hut called the Nurse's Hut. If anyone wasn't very well, they used to go down there. Her main object was to get you back on the field, so she gave you castor oil or syrup of figs. That was it. Mostly you'd get bee stings and things like that. I can remember a time, there were two little boys, and they were poisoned with the berries – deadly nightshade. And they died. They were buried in the churchyard at Yalding and for years after, the parents used to go back to see the graves. The family were there earning money and they couldn't afford to bring the children back. By the time they realised what was wrong with the children it was too late.

The river Medway went near where we were, right behind the farm. And people would go swimming in the Medway. Occasionally you'd get a boy drowned. They were city children but they'd come mostly from round the river Thames. And years ago, boys always swam in the river Thames – it was what they were used to. So, they'd swim and fish in the river Medway.

Eileen O'Sullivan

83

SPIRITUAL MATTERS

Calling the faithful on Sundays at the hop farms

SALVATION ARMY

I remember the Salvation Army were always at the hop-picking. They would have been anti-drink. They used to be in the pubs, in the East End when I grew up. They were always in the pub, coming round with Watchtower and the collecting box, and they'd always do well in East End pubs. Everybody puts in, because they do a lot of good work.

Elaine Jones

There was a place where the Salvation Army were. They would come and mind your baby for you while you worked – they'd charge about a penny a day. They also used to come round the fields in the morning with hot tea – it tasted like washing-up water! They were excellent there, the Salvation Army, they had a first-aid place for us as well.

There was a bevy of Franciscan monks, who wore the brown habits, and they would come round and look after your soul. They used to take the children there for Sunday school. Sometimes they had a magic lantern show for

them. They would do prayers and everybody joined in, even if they weren't strictly religious. The monks would have a bin and come and pick on the field as well. We all used to laugh because they used to say prayers before they ate their lunch. I could always imagine while they're sitting there like that, somebody half-pinching a bit of their food!

Kathleen Ash

THE PRIEST'S TALE

I was a twenty-two year old student in training for the priesthood at the College of the Resurrection, Mirfield. I spent two summers in the Kent hop fields in 1934-5. It is worth noting that a number of the East End Anglo-Catholic priests spent weeks in the hop fields. These were priests who spent their time with people, not in synods and boardrooms. It was an unforgettable experience, those two summers, and the impression remains with me as vivid today as then. I can almost smell again the wood smoke and the penetrating smell of hops. It took weeks to get it out of one's clothes afterwards.

At the turn of the century, those whom the farmer engaged to pick for him had to find their own beds – usually in a cowshed or under a hedge. By the 1930s, the hoppers came to sleep in huts provided for them, huts rather like stables without windows. In the morning, they had to turn out at half-past six. Their breakfast was usually a "slice", that is a slice of bread and a cup of water. Picking began at seven. The Mission sent out barrows of tea and cake on most of the farms at about ten o'clock. It was nothing unusual on a cold morning to sell 24 lbs of slab cake in halfpenny slices and eight or nine gallons of tea in halfpenny cups. The hoppers had a break of half-an-hour at midday and then would pick again until five o'clock.

When the children left the hop gardens at the end of the afternoon, they had nothing to do but to get into mischief, so the Mission ran football and sports and sometimes a "Magic Lantern" show afterwards when it got dark. But most popular of all was "the pictures". The headquarters of the Mission was called The Little Hoppers' Hospital. In front of the Mission was a courtyard which was crammed twice a week with several hundred urchins who came to the Mission movies. One night, as a change from the usual thriller, a film version of "Joan of Arc" was shown. As the flames leapt around the faggots, three hundred voices struck up, "Keep The Home Fires Burning"!

On Saturday night, the courtyard was used for a dance. The songs of the day got sung over and over again. "Little Man, you've had a busy day", "O tell to me Gipsy". The dances served as a good alternative to a "soak" in the Queen's Head.

The Little Hoppers' Hospital dealt with over 300 cases of accident and illness during the three weeks. In addition there was a nurse on most of the farms to deal with minor accidents and injuries – or possibly anything more serious. The greatest dangers were diphtheria, pneumonia – and scalds from boiling water.

Every day, Mass was said in the village church for the student helpers and lady workers and on many outlying farms. It was said in the open air on Sundays. Although there were always more children than adults present at these services, a good attendance of adults was not unknown.

On the village green on Sunday evenings there was a torchlight procession and Mission service. The village signpost served as a pulpit and a piano was taken out of the hall for the hymns. The Bishop of Stepney and other distinguished prelates visited the hop gardens from time to time. One year a certain bishop was walking around the hop garden in his purple cassock when a woman's voice was heard, "Well, I'm jiggered, if it ain't the bleeding Pope!"

Rev. E. George Vince (ret'd)

Thought for the day at Whitbread Hop Farm

Salvation Army service by the huts at Whitbreads

MISSIONARIES

There were always missionaries down round your bin, when you were there. They just used to come and visit the hop-pickers, I don't know why, whether it was conversion, or just to feed the poor. But they were always there, you always had missionaries. And they were most welcome. They picked with you and chatted, and I suppose we all just thought it was just general chat, but there was probably a little bit of propaganda in it about God and what have you. And sometimes they would come and give a service on the field, and preach. People were very respectful then, you know. Now you'd get laughing and giggling and all sorts. But it was a very disciplined life.

Elaine Jones

A ROUGH RIDE

I remember the vicar coming round with tea and buns. He used to call out, "Tea-o! Two-a-penny buns." There was a small hut on the common with a nurse, and she used to see to any scratches or tears. It was mainly little cuts and bruises, nothing untoward, and I never knew of anybody have a fight or anything. But I remember when they took me to see her. I'd gone into a field with another boy and we saw a horse there. I jumped on its back and it ran away with

me. It went towards a little stream at the bottom and I thought I was going in it. I jumped off of the horse and caught my foot in a rut and my ankle came up like a balloon. They had to get a boat to row me across this creek and then take me to the nurse, and she sent me home. That was the first time I'd been on a horse. I found out afterwards that it was a mare in foal.

Harry Demarne

CLOTHES

If we knew a photographer was coming, we'd all look smart. But mostly, we wore old wellingtons; anything we could find. Old coats, old trousers. Where I lived in Hoxton, there was the Hoxton Mission for the very poor, run by Mr German who we all loved. He'd have a mission day when he'd be selling all these clothes that he'd get from grander people that he knew – because he was quite well-to-do, but a very charitable man. He was mainly trying to provide food and shoes for the little kids with nothing, and the people that went hopping would be going there and buying up all this stuff; men's trousers, old jumpers. The big old wooden chest for the hop-picking was being packed all year, practically, from the jumble sales and what have you, "Oh I've got this for hopping." In it went.

Elaine Jones

THE LAST DAY

On the last day, we'd all go over to the old pole puller, Wally Tatters. All the year round he'd be making cider – and what cider! You only wanted the one glass. He had a big wooden vat of the stuff. All the pole pullers would go down and have a drink together on the last day – homedwellers and Londoners. Now the locals knew the stuff and they'd only have one or two glasses. But Danny, my brother-in-law, he liked the taste of this scrumpy – well, it made him delirious! He stripped off and started running round the common naked! Didn't know he was doing it! Everybody was trying to catch him, trying to chuck coats over him. And do you know, when they finished that vat of cider, they found a spanner in it at the bottom! "Oh," said Wally Tatters, "I've been looking for that." When he went to fish it out, the bloody spanner went to dust! That's what the scrumpy had done to it – ate it away and we'd been drinking that!

Tom Easterbrook

The last day would be the best day down there. On the last day, all the men would get the young girls and chuck them in a poke, tie the neck of the poke up, chuck them in the bins and throw hops all over them. It was a good day up there, the last day.

Bet and Tom Easterbrook

September 1931
On the last morning, when we had picked the last field, there was a queer game of catching the women and putting them in the bins. Very likely there will be something about this in the Golden Bough. It is evidently an old custom, and all harvests have some custom of this kind attached to them. The people who were illiterate or thereabouts brought their tally books to me and other "scholars" to have them reckoned up, and some of them paid a copper or two to have it done. I found that in quite a number of cases the farm cashiers had made a mistake in the addition, and invariably the mistake was in favour of the farm. Of course the pickers got the sum due when they complained, but they would not have if they had accepted the farm cashier's reckoning. Moreover, the farm had a mean little rule that anyone who was going to complain about his tally book had to wait till all the other pickers had been paid off. This meant waiting till the afternoon, so that some people who had buses to catch had to go home without claiming the sum due to them. (Of course it was only a few coppers in most cases. One woman's book, however, was added up over £1 wrong.)

George Orwell, Collected Essays

Hoppers in the bin, a last day ritual (photo lent by Dot Seadon)

They chucked my father off the hop farm once, it was November. He was supposed to have gone home about the middle of October. He wouldn't go home! In the end, the farmer said, "You've got to vacate the hut, Mr Bowers, there's cattle going in there." But he didn't want to come home, he would have spent Christmas there, he liked it so much!

Albert Bowers

By "The Bell" there was an orchard, and you always went for your apples, cookers. They were real hopping apples. When you got home, you'd give your neighbours hopping apples that you'd bought down there. And you'd have a nice meal of chicken, roast chicken really in those days was a real luxury. It wasn't the cheapest meat you could buy, not like it is today. You used to go round and pick a chicken out and they would have it killed for you.

Kathleen Ash

You'd all finish work on the Friday. You always had somebody to come and fetch you. I think they used to charge you ten shillings in those days to take you and bring you back in the lorry. It all depended on the lorry driver, when he could get down there. If he couldn't get down there until Saturday evening, you'd wait until Saturday evening. But you had to be off the field by the weekend; you weren't allowed to stay any longer. When we came back from hop-picking, we were always brown, but we had to have our hair cropped short at the back ... because of

nits. The first thing back at school was, "Come out here and have your head checked, make sure you didn't bring anything home with you!".

Laura Murphy

I loved it when we came home. My mum would always bring home a couple of fresh chickens. We used to go to the farm and we used to bring them home with the feathers on. They just used to hang by their legs. I used to go scrumping with my sister. We used to have a pillow case full of what we called hopping apples and big king cooking apples. Mum used to make apple pies, apple dumplings. It used to be wonderful when we came home because of all the things that we brought with us. I suppose, looking back now, it was because everything was so fresh.

Joan Clarkson

At the end of hop-picking, we always had a cooked dinner for the pickers. I used to make a meat pudding, potatoes and cabbage, and have a sweet at the end. The hop-pickers used to have a sing-song and then my husband used to take them back to Tonbridge station with their bits of luggage and everything and that was the end of the hop-picking time. It was all quiet and peace; it was terrible! I missed them, I really did. But I always used to say to the Londoners, "It's all right you coming down to pick – you want to come and train them; you wouldn't want the job so quick then!" because it really was hard work, training hops.

Alice Heskitt

An end of hopping party at Whitbread's

Public events were celebrated by hop-pickers at Whitbread Hop Farm

My Dad had had his orders before we went away! He had to paint the kitchen and put some new wallpaper on the living room, so when we came back, it felt quite posh, because everything was nice and comfortable.

Laura Murphy

When it was time to come home you could go to the farmer and buy a bushel of lovely big hopping apples and you would bring some hops home. This would all be hanging up at the end of the lorry, with your chickens – you'd bring back a couple of chickens. We used to sing as we went:-

When we go down hopping
Hopping down in Kent ...

I can't think of all the words now! But we used to sing on the lorries, taking us back and forward. The day before we came home, the homedwellers would send their kids round to see what we had left ... they were on the scrounge for what we left – wasn't much, believe me! Mum used to say, "Yeah, they soon know who their friends are when they want anything!" They were glad of our boots, so I think they must have been hard up.

Laura Murphy

You didn't have a party as such. You went to the farm office to get your money when you were finished picking. Maybe you'd be there for one or two more days, which gave you time to pack up to come home. But then, all those that were in the little area where you were, you went and had a drink together at "The Bell". But you knew you were going to see them all next year. Nobody had thought that you wouldn't go, or for any reason that you would be dead or something like that. No, nobody'd thought that. And the following year the day you arrived you spent saying, "Oh hello!"

Kathleen Ash

On the way home, Swanley would be half way, and we'd stop there. Of course, everyone had their money, coming home, so they'd be drinking and singing! As time went on and we became more affluent, we'd come home by lorry. You'd see the lorries with chickens hanging off the back, where they'd bought them off the farm. And you always brought back a bunch of hops. Everyone did. Even though they'd been picking them for six weeks, they still came home with their hops! We'd stop at "The Bull" in Birchwood. That was the half-way landmark, everybody knew it. It's still there. It was like a meeting place. The children used to run wild and the fathers and mothers would be drinking. Then you came up the road through Wrotham Hill.

Bill O'Sullivan

On the last day you all had to go and line up with your book – you had the tally book – and all chattering and everybody working out what they've got. And the parents'd be paying their children out the money for the work they'd done – because you get paid at the end of the hop-picking. Although people were allowed to sub if they were really hard up. There was just a great feeling of friendliness and happiness; a lot of fun. It was lovely. And even the farmer and all the farmhands were jovial and everything. The farmer would thank you. Mr Mainwaring was terribly middle class, you know, a posh farmer, he was not your oo-arr farmer, and he'd come and thank the people. He was always around. He'd stalk along the farm with his stick and speak to us, come along and see what was going on, how the other half lived. In fact one girl that we used to go hopping with – she was a real laugh – she ended up marrying the farmer. She was a real card. She was about eighteen, and she married a wealthy farmer of about forty. She used to pick and she ended up in the gracious living.

Elaine Jones

HOME-DWELLERS' VIEWS

PREPARATIONS IN KENT

Before the hop-pickers came down, the farmer used to go to all the huts, and they used to spray lime, wash them out with lime, and they used to leave so many faggots – that's a bundle of wood – for their beds. They'd put say eight faggots in and a couple of bails of straw. And that was their beds. I used to think, rather them than me, because hops used to upset me, and the hop smell went into everything, you couldn't get away from it. It got on to peoples' clothes and you had a job to get your hands clean. I don't think you did get your hands clean in those days, they stayed dirty. Terrible gunge and stuff, there's a powder in the hops.

Daphne Wallace

DRYING THE HOPS

My grandfather was a hop drier. The drying was done in an oast house. The hops were dried on coal, on well steamed coal; it didn't give a flame, just glowed. He was a drier, which was a very well paid job, because it was seven days a week, twenty four hours a day, you didn't stop; once it started it went all the time.

The hops came in straight away to be dried. They were dried and packed and within three or four days they were loaded in these long bags or "pockets", as they were known, loaded on to wagons, taken to the train at Hawkhurst station and then they were away to the hop exchange.

Leslie Kemp

When they used to dry the hops I used to help. In the oast house they had a big net, made of sacking, very heavy sacking. You'd go in there with nothing on your feet and you shovelled the hops over with your feet, to turn them. But as you looked down, you could see this great big fire! But you wouldn't fall through it or anything because it was strong sacking! The blokes who used to dry the hops never had any sleep – they stayed awake all day and all night, because you had certain times for the hops to come out, so that they weren't dried too much. Then they had to go into big sacks and then a man comes with what they call a presser and then they take a sample away to let you know if the hops were good. Because in them days you had them for beer. Now they use the hops mostly for dyes.

Alice Heskitt

BLAMED FOR EVERYTHING

Londoners always got blamed for things that went on in the country, stealing apples or chickens, and things like that, but often it wasn't the Londoners, it was just local people stealing and they blamed it on the Londoners. It happened quite a lot. Somebody would miss about half a dozen chicken, and it'd be, "Them Londoners were round last night." And you knew it wasn't them really. My father always used to say, "It wasn't the Londoners because they wouldn't know how to kill it." Some of them, if there were cows in the fields, they walked miles to avoid cows and things like that. I don't think they called them cows, they was always bulls, and they were frightened of bulls.

I used to find it exciting as a village child when I saw the netting going up in front of the counters in the local shops, because then I knew the hop-picking would soon start. The shopkeepers put wire netting all round the front of the shop because they thought the Londoners would pinch. The local people always went round the back, and of course they were doing the same thing. There was more things stolen during hop-picking than there was all the year round because the local people knew they could get away with it.

Daphne Wallace

MAKING A FORTUNE OUT OF THE LONDONERS

During the week, it was mainly women and children down here, as the men had jobs in London, but they came down at weekends. Somebody'd have a lorry, or they'd hire one, and they used to be sitting on the floor, or standing up in the lorry, husbands, sons, sons-in-law, from all the different families and then the pubs were crowded out. The roads would be packed with people walking to the pub or walking home. You'd hear them singing until late at night.

I used to love the Londoners because I made a fortune on their glasses. All the public houses in this area used to be one room for the locals. Every other room they put barrels of beer in the windows and served all the Londoners through the hatches. I was ten years of age. A pint of beer then was 4d and they used to charge a shilling deposit on the glasses, although they only cost them about 2d. The Londoners used to buy the glass you see and every time they wanted a refill they used to keep their glass. There was no way you could cope as it was, serving out of windows everywhere to keep them going. There was a queue at these hatches for beer all night long.

So when the Londoners went home to their huts, naturally all the local boys were out collecting all the glasses and getting something back on them. They marked the glasses on the bottom, and you had to take them back to the same pub to collect the deposit. Every publican in this area would say the same; five weeks of hopping, no need to open the rest of the year, he'd made enough.

Bill Slack

A LOCAL VIEW

I was born in a hop village where hops were grown, so I saw the thing, not from the hop-pickers' angle, but from the angle of the people who received the hop-pickers. I was a farm labourer's son and I watched what was going on. Local school holidays were adjusted to fit in with the hop-picking. We didn't go back to school until the end of September, the beginning of October. That would have been the return to school of the hop-picking villagers.

There was a feeling of general expectation. It was as though the people coming down from London were coming down from Mars. And they came down every year when the hops were ready for picking, mainly from the East End of London, mainly dockers' families, I think.

They all came down on a special train from London Bridge, carrying everything with them. The farmer would fetch them from the station with his wagon and horses. All their stuff would be thrown on the wagon, and the kids and the women would jump on the wagon, and if there were any men they'd usually walk behind or with the wagon. There was a general atmosphere of festivity about it. It was exciting, yes, I think it was exciting. It was something different.

The hop-pickers' huts were just like a room. There was just one room for a family and they all slept in there. A week before they came, the farm workers would be putting straw in there for them to sleep on. The huts were normally in an open-ended square and they would build a great fire for them in the middle of this square. Usually the farm workers would have got it going for them, and when they arrived, they arrived with their bedding and their pots and pans and everything and they would generally all get together and cook on the middle of this thing. It was their holiday, you see, getting them out into the air.

In the hop garden itself, the picking was done by the people who'd come from London. They would be picking in one section and any local pickers would be picking in another section. And the Londoners would be referred to as the 'Oppers – over the 'Oppers' section, as they called it – and the people from the village who were doing it would be kown as the Home Pickers. There was this differentiation between them which in later life, I came to see for what it really was.

Kids were expected to pick in the morning. They would usually have a little basket or an umbrella to pick into. In the afternoon they'd let them go to play. Then they would clear off out of the hop field into the woods, that sort of thing.

The women and children would pick all the week and on Friday or Saturday they would draw the money that they'd earned and their husbands would join them. The money would be transferred down the pub, while the kids hung about outside. I remember the kids standing outside the pub with glasses of lemonade and packets of crisps being handed out to them.

The pubs were altered. The class system in Britain being what it is, there had to be a differentiation. And the normal public bar of the pub would have a big notice over it saying, "Hop Pickers Only." And the local people, who would normally be in the public bar would go somewhere else. The Londoners were noisy and the locals didn't want their ambience disturbed, so they were kept separate.

Local shopkeepers would stock everything they could get rid of. It was their boom season. Local people would tell stories about them: "Good lord, did you hear what they did last night?" – things like that. I suppose if there were any crimes in the neighbourhood it would be put down to them. It was very convenient.

But really they were very law abiding. The worst thing they did – if there was a worst thing – was make a noise on a Saturday night. I used to lie in bed with the window open and, because we lived in the centre of the village, I could hear them go from the pub to a farm a mile away where their huts were. They sang all the way, songs like "Nelly Dean", songs about London and all the songs that people sing when they've had too much to drink.

Leslie Kemp

Stringing the hops (photo lent by John Wardley)

91

The Tally Man (photo lent by Whitbread Hop Farm)

many bines from one heel. We trained the new shoots up in about April, the end of April. You put nine bines up the pole and you tie them with rushes that you'd picked and dried the summer before. But you had to make sure you'd got it all tied up! You train hops the opposite way to runner beans: anti-clockwise. There could be thousands of bines to do and you had to do nine hundred of them tied over three times before you got thirty shillings. And I don't mind admitting, I cried many a time, because having two children with me in the field, I'd be well behind the other women. I just rushed to and fro. The other ladies' children were grown up and going to school, but I had two kids to pull around in a pram and what with feeding them and everything, I know what hard work is. I used to go out four o'clock in the morning to catch up. My husband would look after the boys while I was gone. He had to be at work at seven, so I'd take a clock with me and be home by seven o'clock for him to go to work.

We'd have to put the wire and string up for the bines to grow up. We'd both be on stilts, because my husband would pull the wire to the next pole and I used to hand him the round hook things to fix the wire, and after that was done, I used to feed the wire with these hooks to my husband. After that was all done that's when you'd put up the string. A man does that job. He has the ball of string in his apron and he goes along with a long hook to reach up to

I married a farm worker who worked on a hop farm in Tonbridge – Grange Farm. When I first started, I'd never known farm work, but I suppose I accepted it. It was very hard. I used to go to work at eight o'clock in the morning, and come home at midday, light a kitchen fire to fry bubble and squeak and have a piece of bacon with it, and we had to be out on the fields again at one o'clock. Then we used to come home at five o'clock and I used to have to cook a proper dinner for ourselves – you always cooked enough so that you could have a little left over for lunch the next day. Then there was the childrens' washing to do, bath them, and get them to bed.

On Saturday afternoons, I used to walk from Grange Farm to Tonbridge, which was nearly five miles, to do my shopping. And I used to do two lots of baking a week. I used to do jam, bottle all my fruit, everything. You could open the pantry and the boys would say, "Mum can we have some cherries today?" or, "Can we have some pears today?" I worked on the farm haystacking, which is very heavy work and I had to learn to milk cows. And threshing is the filthiest job on earth – the machine would throw all the dust and stuff out at you.

We had poles for hop training in those days. In February, the men cut the heel of the hop, that's the hard root. They move the dirt away and they cut a slice into the root and that starts the new hopshoots to grow. You'd get ever so

The stilt man erects the wires for the hops to grow up (photo lent by Whitbread Hop Farm)

Keeping the cold out (photo lent by John Wardley)

Stringing the hop (photo lent by John Wardley)

the wire, then down to the heel, where there is a type of skewer, but bigger. All the hop bines would be around that and you've got four strings going up to the wire. Up that string you put three bines on one string and two bines up to the other one. You had to make sure the bines were close to the string, because the men would go along with the tractor with a shimmer and he would plough them out, then you wouldn't have any hops. In them days if you were working on a farm where there was hops, it was more important for a woman to do the hop-training because the men were doing other work and couldn't spare their time to train. After that you pull all the bines away from the heel and then you strip them half way up to let the air go through. When I was hop tying, it made my fingers very very sore, dreadful, it really takes the skin off the back of your fingers. You could get quite bad cuts on the palms of your hands. But when we were stripping the bines, we always wore gloves, that's why we used to ask everybody for old gloves. Some farmers didn't bother to strip the bines, but our boss always did. Hop bines grow right down and with the thick leaves, it would be like a bush; that's why you'd have to strip them so that air can get right through.

The bines would have to have grown over the top of the wire by June 21st. That gives you an idea when the hops are ready, not actually the hops but the bines, themselves should be over the top of the wires by June 21st – midsummer. If they're not, its going to be a late hop-picking.

You can get a terrible hop blight which is called the red spider. If you get blight, you cannot go on that hop garden at all unless you wash your wellingtons and clothes with disinfectant; you change your clothes and leave them in a

tent in the field and they're all left there because if the blight spread, it could kill all the hops. We'd string that diseased bine right off so nobody could get in there. We had to cut those bines down and burn them straight away before the blight travelled.

Nothing more was done in the hop garden after that, until the Londoners came. Then my husband used to go with a horse and cart to Tonbridge station and pick some of the Londoners up with their bits of furniture what they used to bring. In Tonbridge, there is a pub called The Mitre, and the Londoners taught this horse to drink a pint of beer. So he automatically used to go into The Mitre when he came back from the station with the Londoners. The horse would have his pint and then off he'd go up to the farm.

Alice Heskitt

LONDON – ANOTHER WORLD

We could never afford to go up to London. The first time I went up to London was when I had my own children. I took them up to see Buckingham Palace. I can't ever remember going up before that. I think my youngest son was four or five. He's thirty-five now. Nowadays people think nothing of just going up to London for a day's shopping.

Daphne Wallace

THE WAR YEARS

The year the war started, 1939, one of my mum's sisters had a baby, and her husband was so worried that he said, "Go and stay with your mum and be safe." Because you didn't really know it was going to be the phoney war; you thought you were going to be invaded, or there were going to be parachutists; there were all sorts of rumours. He thought she would be safer really in the country, so she came down to Kent with the baby. It's very rough ground in the hop gardens, very difficult to push a pram. My mum went and got an orange box from the fruit sellers, put feather pillows in it, and used the cot blanket. She used to take Brian out to the fields in an orange box, and put a big umbrella up, to keep the sun and rain off him.

We were down hopping when the war broke out. I was blackberry-picking. We used to go down by the river Medway – there was always a lot of people fishing down there. We used to like to go down there; there was, I think it was a weir, which used to fascinate me. But there were lots of blackberry bushes and we used to go blackberry-picking. It was Sunday, so we had our nicest clothes, but like most children we didn't think about that when we decided to pick blackberries. We heard the siren but we didn't know what it was. I was nine, my sister was fourteen, and she didn't know what it was. We were all down there picking blackberries.

My gran'd heard on somebody's radio that the war had started, and she cried. She remembered the 1914–18 war of course. She cried and she was so worried because she didn't know where we were. When we came back, we all got a slap! She was so worried.

She was a terrific character my gran. She couldn't bear you to giggle, so every now and again if you kept giggling and she didn't know what you were laughing about, and especially if you were all in a row, you'd get one big mighty slap and you all got a piece of it.

We were going to go straight back to London when war was declared, but then we decided not to. My school had already gone away. So my father thought we would be better off in Kent than in London. So we stayed. I remember going out to the fields, I think it was the next day, and the air raid siren went, and a 'plane came over.

It was only one 'plane, and it was English anyway, but my grandmother threw us all in the ditch to protect us. Fortunately it was dry. She knelt on the green verge, and she got out her rosary and she was saying the Hail Mary. She never thought that she could be machine-gunned or anything.

After that, I was evacuated. My gran went hop-picking during the war, I'm sure she did. I don't remember going again myself until 1944. We went down for a weekend, when my mother's sister got married. She got married at home, on the Friday, and we went down Saturday and came home Sunday. I don't think I ever went again apart from that. It was just the same as I remembered it. Probably even nicer, because I was older. I was with my sister, and my mum's youngest sister and a friend of hers. I was fourteen, they were nineteen. And I was allowed to go out with them.

Joan Clarkson

'Ma' Barnett's Ultimatum:

A 'SQUIRT' LIKE HITLER CAN'T STOP HOP-PICKING

Cover From Bombers At Hand

WAR or no war, Mrs. Mary Ann Barnett, from Brixton Hill, London, is not to be denied her annual hop-picking holiday.

With blankets and clothes and tinned foods and torch and ration book an' all, she arrived at Beltring in the Weald of Kent this week.

Twenty bushels of good quality hops were picked by her nimble fingers ere the first day of he. "long vacation" had elapsed. When she really gets going Mrs. Barnett can pick 40 bushels a day.

"At three bushels a bob that's about 13 shillings a day," she told a "Kent Messenger" reporter.

HITLER CAN'T STOP HER

"I first came here when I was a fortnight old, and in all my 54 years I have missed coming only twice.

"**A squirt like Hitler's not going to spoil my holiday. Besides 'hubby' looks like being out of work, and the money's handy.**

"I've only brought Alma, my youngest daughter, with me this year. She is 10, and is enjoying herself."

MORE PEACEFUL THAN EVER

Strangely enough the hop gardens seem more peaceful than ever. There are not nearly so many pickers as usual, and consequently a lot of the boisterous spirit is missing.

Last year they were singing "The Lambeth Walk" at the top of their voices. This year they talk about the air raids over London.

They've had air raid alarms themselves, but took them calmly.

WAPPING SAFE—SO FAR AS WE KNOW

"Hop picking is very tiring, said Mrs. Barnett. "Last night we heard the sirens and heavy gunfire, but we all stayed in our huts and most of us fell off to sleep. It's safer here than in London."

"Any damage at Wapping?" asked red-armed, stout Mrs. Harris, another doyen of the hop gardens, who was disappointed when I couldn't enlighten her, for the simple reason that Wapping has not been in my visiting itinerary of late.

READY TO GO TO SHELTER

If the hop pickers hear the sirens in day time they take cover in specially prepared trenches. The hops are being picked in a different order than usual so that pickers are always handy to the dugouts. They can then hide quickly.

BROUGHT HER WARDEN'S WHISTLE

The hop gardens have their own A.R.P. units ready for emergency, and these can count on the help, too, of 10-years-old Mary Catchsides, from Rotherhithe. Mary has been a part-time warden for two years, and has brought her whistle, civilian duty respirator, steel helmet and warrant card along with her.

The other night, she gave a "rift" Rotherhithe "rousing" to a Bermondsey man who shone his torch during an air raid.

MORE WORK FOR THEM

The Catchsides, incidentally, have come down in full force. There are 11 of them altogether, and they have six bins between them. Not bad going considering that this year there are only 360 bins being filled, compared with the customary 900.

"That means more hops for us to pick, and a longer stay here," said Mrs. H. Catchsides, head of the Catchsides contingent.

HER "OLD MAN" IS PINING

"My old man's almost breaking his heart," she added. "He's a stevedore at the docks, and has been out of work a bit lately.

"**Stack my eye if he didn't have to work on Sunday after he'd got already to come down here. He'll be along at the week-end to see us.**"

"Would that there were even more Catchsides," sighed the manager as he looked along the avenues of hops waiting to be picked.

Youngest visitor to the gardens is the five-months-old baby of Mr. and Mrs. Jim Mahoney, of Brixton.

FAMILY OF FIVE WITH THEM

Mr. and Mrs. Mahoney have a family of five with them. Jim was working on the Underground, but recently had a serious illness.

"I have come down for a cheap holiday so that I can recuperate," he said. "This place agrees with the kiddies."

Asked how they were managing for food, Mrs. Mahoney said: "Okedoke. We have brought our emergency ration cards with us, and the butcher comes round every day. We stocked ourselves well with tinned foods before leaving."

HAVING A GREAT TIME

On the next bin, picking away quickly, yet by no means expertly, were two youths from Bermondsey, Charlie Mack and Wally Salisbury. They gave up their London jobs when they heard that hop pickers were required. Their pal, Wally Bygraves, is a hop puller. The three share the same hut, and are having a great time.

"Might as well get used to camp life before we go in the Army," Charlie commented drily. He, like his chums, is 18.

SHORTAGE MADE GOOD

With many of the old-timers staying at home this year villagers have come to the farmers' aid by taking a large number of bins. They are working together in the same set.

Some, owing to shortage of men, are acting as binmen, and they include pretty Margaret Bishop, aged 18, of Yalding. Wearing long blue trousers with juniper to tone, her blonde hair kept tidy by a net. Margaret looked very businesslike as she wielded the long hop puller, and then fiercely cut through the bines with a jack knife.

If Margaret is typical of the "binmen" I rather envy Charlie Mack and Co. They will agree without doubt that even war has its compensations.

Fagg's Hurricane Batting

Arthur Fagg, England and Kent, hit 101 off 32 balls in 18 minutes in a cricket match in the Hastings district last week. He hit seven 6's. A Kent, amateur, B. H. Valentine, has also been doing some big hitting. Playing for Aldershot Command, Valentine reached three figures on Saturday in less than an hour.

A WAR-TIME WEDDING

My husband was a Reservist in 1939, so he knew he'd be one of the first to get his calling up papers. We had had our banns read in St. Mary's Church, Plaistow, to get married at the end of September, and we were getting a flat ready to move into by then.

On Saturday 2nd September, the lorry was outside to take my mum and all the family hop-picking down at Marden in Kent. My mum loved her hop-picking. She'd never miss that. We used to take everything barring the kitchen sink.

I was clearing up after they'd gone, scrubbing the passage, when my husband-to-be came in. "Come on", he said, "we're getting married. I'm expecting me papers any minute." I was flabbergasted. I said, "But we got our banns read in the church. How can we do it?" He said, "I'll go down to the vicar and ask his opinion." The vicar told him he'd have to phone through to Westminster Abbey to get a special licence and we'd have to go up there to the Sanctuary to collect it. When he came back and told me that, we went round to see my brother. He had a greengrocer's business, but he just shut up the shop there and then, fetched out the car and he and his wife took us to Westminster. We never even knew where it was. We just parked the car in a cul-de-sac, got out and asked somebody the way. They said, "You've parked just in front of it."

When we opened the door, there was a doorman stacking all the sandbags up. He said, "Are you the couple from St. Mary's? Well, don't wait your turn because you won't get back to the church in time. When the next couple come down from upstairs, you go straight up." When he opened the door, we had a shock. There were couples lining up all up the stairs. They were all wanting a special licence because of the crisis. None of the other couples said anything to us when we went straight in. We got the licence and got back to the church just in time; any later and they wouldn't have been allowed to marry us.

There wasn't a soul in the church, just the four of us. My brother gave me away and my sister-in-law was best man. I think I must have been the first woman that had a woman for best man! That was because all the rest of the family, everybody, had already gone to the hop fields. We never had a bouquet, not even a button-hole, nothing. As I got up from the altar I looked down and I had a ladder right down the back of my stockings. We came back and had kippers for tea at my sister's.

On the Sunday, the day after, my brother decided to take a lorry load of fruit down to the hop fields to sell, and we went with him, the first day of our honeymoon! We were going along when all of a sudden, the sirens went. War was declared. Please take cover. So instead of getting off and taking cover, my brother got off and covered all the fruit and vegetables over! Anyway, we saw my mum and explained it all to her, and she was quite all right about it. Every year since then, on 2nd September, I buy myself a bouquet of flowers to make up for the one I never had on my wedding day.

Florence Burgess

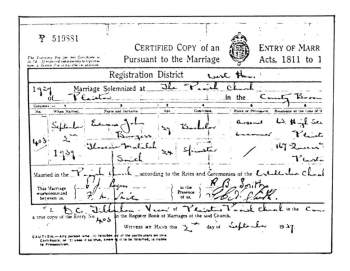

Florence Burgess's wedding certificate

I went picking until the war started and then I got called up. I knew I was going to be called up, but I informed them that I wouldn't be at home when my papers come but I'd be down the hop country. And they sent them down there to me, at the farm, and I got called up from there. Would I come back to Downham, would I go to a certain place in Downham to get my Land Army uniform, and would I go to the bottom of Downham Way and meet another girl who would also be in uniform; you wear your uniform, she will wear her uniform, meet outside Woolworths at Downham Way, this is the address where she lives, she's got yours, please write to her or ring her and make yourself so that you can identify each other when you got there. And her name was Daisy and we stayed together the whole four years in the war.

And guess where I was put. I was put threshing the corn on the harvester, and when that corn was cut and we were looking for a job, I was put back on the hop-field, training the hops round the bines. The hops go from right to left round the string. And you train them up clockwise right to the top. If you're left handed and you go that way round, when you come back in the morning, they're all undone. Because they come in with the sun. They just unwind themselves right off the string.

Then, when the corn was ready to be cut, to be threshed, we had to get back on the machines. There was a man, Mr Jones that owned this threshing machine. The farmers used to hire his machine for three days at a time to get the corn cut. And four of us girls were employed by this Mr Jones. We were all issued with bikes, and we went with the machine. But when we got to that farmer, perhaps us four girls on that machine and a couple of men wasn't enough, so the dairy girls used to come and help us. And if that wasn't enough they used to call the army in.

We were trained to pick up potatoes and to do the ground work. We had a lovely time, we really did. If I hadn't been engaged to be married, I don't think I'd have come out.

Marjorie Balcombe

AN EVACUEE REMEMBERS

I can remember in the street when the people opposite who had a large family were getting ready to go and it was a very big lorry, and literally, everything was hooked on, frying pans, saucepans, and great big mattresses. Feather mattresses rather than the big palliasse things that they had on the farm. People must have taken their own mattresses. It was lovely watching them getting ready to go, it really was. They were my schoolfriends. I think it might have been holiday time, the school holiday time. I think it possibly overlapped. I remember them getting ready to go – it was the Ellis family, before the war, 1936, 1937. And then when that street was bombed on that first bombing raid in September 1940, when so much damage was done, we never had any further contact. I don't know where they went.

I went hop-picking several times during the war, as I was evacuated with a family that did it regularly. It was just their autumn job to go hop-picking at the farm. They needed the money to supplement their income. He was a coalman, the local coalman. I don't remember her working at all, she must have stayed at home to look after us. It was just the women and children helping with the hops. I don't remember seeing any men except those that weighed up the measures, the actual farm labourers.

The "homedwellers" lived in their own homes, but went every day to a local farm at Pembury. We were picked up by a horse and cart and taken to the hop field.

We took sandwiches for lunch, beetroot sandwiches. I can taste it now! I can see the red of the beetroot coming through the bread now. And we had these filthy fingers, your filthy hands. When you picked hops you got the sticky brown green, black greenish stuff on them that stuck, so that when you ate the sandwiches you were also tasting this stuff. It didn't come off on the sandwiches, but you had the smell of it on your fingers that actually went on to your bread. We had cold cocoa in a lemonade bottle. It was made with water, very dark, very sweet, very cold.

You'd get paid by the bushel. I think we got 6d a bushel. I know one wonderful time, I had my own bin and the money that I picked and earned it was mine, so that you picked for the day and that was wonderful. That was my own money. But you were not allowed leaves and it was very tempting to put your leaves in to make the weight; but they're aware of it and you had to clear all the leaves out of the basket before they measured it for you. They scooped it up and then it'd be transferred into great big hopping sacks that were all of six foot tall. And at the end of the day – or earlier if you could, you called out to them, "Empty the bin!" because you'd filled the bin up before anyone else did.

I was about thirteen the year I had my own bin, well half a bin really. It was six feet long and quite deep. I know you would be hanging over the side trying to get the leaves out. Picking hops could be very uncomfortable. You pulled the bines down and they were very wet and you'd be all scratched from the bines that were coming onto your arm, you'd scratch and you'd get chaps. But on the other hand, if it was very hot, then you always seemed to get beetles and things crawling down you and fleas. We took them home with us. Whether it was the hay making season, when it was fleas anyway, or whether it was just hop-picking that was fleas, you were itching with bites. So either way it was quite uncomfortable, and I can remember picking with bare arms which was a mistake.

We worked from eight o'clock to five. I know you were very tired and if you'd said, "Oh, I want my own bin," then no way could you slip off, but you wanted to by about three in the afternoon.

Normally, children might not have been picking all day, but they would certainly have helped in the morning, "Come on, you pick for a couple of hours, and then you can go off and play."

I'm not sure what I bought with my money. It might have been about two shillings. I probably bought a book or two, because sweets were hard to come by and you couldn't get many clothes. I might have bought a savings stamp. I had my own book then. In my card, and when your card was full up you could take it to the post office and it was worth fifteen shillings. That's what I would have done. In fact I had it for a very long time actually, that fifteen shillings and I've still got a card with a stamp on it now.

Joan Pearce

In 1940, September, during the war, we were bombed out of our house, so we decided to go hop-picking at Three Chimneys Farm. We were all busy picking when suddenly all hell broke loose. German planes were machine gunning us and my mum, God rest her soul, was eighteen stone and a cripple in a wheel chair. But she wouldn't budge from her bin so we had to put an old tin bath over her head. Her comment was "no German b– is going to stop me from filling my bin." So the rest of us took shelter in the dugouts provided by the farmer. No one was hurt, thank God, and that was the only incident.

After the war I went up to the hop huts with a family from Bermondsey and I went back to live with them until I got re-housed by the council because I got bombed out.

Kit O'Connell

I was at Whitbread's during the Blitz. I didn't take a bin that year because I was so heavily pregnant, but I went down with my mother, for a holiday really. The day we went, the Blitz started, September 7th. My husband had got an unexpected holiday – he was working at Woolwich Arsenal in the high explosives department, and they had worked full out through the summer. We got to Whitbread's and before tea time the bombers were going over, and bombed Surrey Docks where I came from. That night all I heard was the bombers going over. Thank God, I wasn't there. I was going to have the baby at home, so going away as late as September 7th – I was due at the end of September – all the clean curtains were up, everything was ready for when I came back. Well, the curtains were ripped to smithereens, and no windows were left!

Down at Whitbread's, there was fighting going on overhead all the time, and there were planes brought down there. But it wasn't quite so bad as being in London where you were a target. My mother said, "Well you'd best stay." So off I toddled up to Pembury Hospital, and they said, "Oh yes, that's fine. If your labour starts, you come here." On the last day when the picking had finished everybody went to the local pub, "The Bell", to have a drink, and say goodbye until next year. I was there with my little girl of three, my husband, and I think my younger sisters, when – I started! It was about ten o'clock and they were all leaving the pub. The farm manager, a Mr Waghorn, and my husband went to phone for an ambulance. When the ambulance came, they said they had to make a big detour because there were unexploded bombs. I said, "I've got an unexploded bomb!" We got to the hospital in the early hours of the Friday morning, but Michael wasn't born until the evening, until twenty past six.

The next day, everybody had gone home, and I didn't get any visitors all the week. My husband was back at work, he couldn't afford the fare back down anyway. The lady in the next bed was a local lady and she felt so sorry for me, she gave me two bars of chocolate. When Michael was ten days old, I came home and then had to make some arrangements to be evacuated. I don't know if it's because he was born down there, but my son Michael always loved hop-picking. He wishes with all his heart that there were places around today where you could still go to pick hops.

I went back to Whitbread's again directly the war was over. I went every year until one year there was a big hop failure; the crops failed, and Whitbread's put names in a hat and pulled so many out. Mine wasn't one of them, nor my mother, who'd been going there for a long time. That's just one of those things. But we went to another farm at Matfield.

Kathleen Ash

My aunt nearly had all her teeth blown out, when the bombs was going off going hopping. She'd just got off the van, just arrived there, and everyone ran with the bombs being dropped, and she didn't run in time and she got caught by the blast and it knocked all her teeth out. And she lost her sense of smell, and she's never got it back.

Hilary Irving

Trench shelters being dug for hop-pickers
(photo lent by Whitbread Hop Farm)

A NARROW ESCAPE

During the war, my nephew Jimmy came down to the hop fields in his uniform, he had his pack, gun, everything. Well, that night, about six of us went down the pub. On the way back, we passed where the toilets were and someone said to Jimmy, "Let's see you shoot that gun, see if you can hit that toilet hut over there." So he got his gun out and I said, "Wait a minute, don't shoot yet, old Mr Riley might be there." – that was the old man that always used to be in the toilets, there was something wrong with him. Well, I was right, Old Riley was in there! If Jimmy had shot at that hut, it would have hit him right in the head and killed him stone dead.

Mike Fitzgerald

ESCAPE FROM BOMBING

I recall how, during the early and mid 1940s, we travelled to the Kentish hop fields, for at least four consecutive years. "We" consisted of Gran, (the leader, motivator and instigator of the whole scene) my mother, brother and sister. Occasionally we would acquire the odd aunt or uncle who would join the family for the hop-picking season. Hop-picking was considered by many as a means of escaping the traumas of London life at the time when we were still enduring regular air raids.

Conditions at the farm were appalling. The accommodation was a row of timber huts with tin roofs. No light, no heat and the only water came from the communal tap in the field. Cooking was done on an open fire by means of faggots which were bundles of burnable twigs. If you owned a simple primus stove, you were privileged! You could cook early morning porridge without leaving the hut. Toilets were holes in the ground, treated occasionally with chemicals.

Despite all this, many of the families were regular hop-pickers, travelling down mostly from East and South London. I recall the Kellys from the Elephant and Castle, the Reeves family from Walworth Road and families from Charlton, Welling, Greenwich whose names I can't now recall, but they would reappear every year.

Tony Whytock

MRS. ANNIE MANKLOW, of Wouldham, who this year has completed 50 years of hopping at Chartham. She told a "Kent Messenger" reporter that it would take more than Hitler to prevent her taking what she has for half a century regarded as her annual holiday. She has had ten children and when she first came to work in the Chartham hop gardens she brought with her her first-born, then 7 months old. As a proof of her contempt for Hitler she continued picking the hops for this picture while an air-battle raged overhead.

We were evacuated to Kent during the War, because London had the heavy bombing. Of all places to go to avoid the bombs! We were worse off because they were coming over Kent! The Battle of Britain was all fought over Kent. And we were there. The Spitfires were fighting all round you. I was sixteen or seventeen. I didn't care really, because I didn't realise the danger. "Oh there's another one coming down." "Is that one of ours?" And you'd see the Spitfires all going up to the German bombers and you'd see one plane come down. We had one Spitfire came down on the farm, shot down. Everybody rushed over and of course it was in flames. I can remember everybody running to where the Spitfire came down. But there was nothing to be done, it was all just one big blaze.

Eileen O'Sullivan

During the war we used to get leave from work to go hop-picking, because it was essential work ... we would be allowed a pass to travel and get so many weeks off our other war work. In 1944, we went hop-picking but we didn't know it was in the middle of Doodlebug Alley! That was where the doodlebugs came over from France: there were so many brought down in Kent, they called it "Doodlebug Alley". There was a military station at Swanley, on the way down to the farm and we had to show them the pass sent by the farmer saying that he needed us there on his farm to pick the hops.

Charlotte Fowler

They'd make a sort of a buzzing noise, the doodlebugs, and then all of a sudden it would stop. Then you knew it was on its way down ... there wasn't any shelter in the hop fields, except in the hop bin! Underneath the hop bin! If you saw it coming this way, you'd run that way!

Vi Lewis

One day during the war, we had sixty two bombs drop on our farm! There was one crater which would take three doubledecker buses. You see, when the bombers didn't get to London, they turned and they used to drop their bombs on Kent, so they didn't have to travel back with them. Once, I had all my windows blown out. We carried on with the work in the fields, but it wasn't safe really. When you heard the air raid siren, you all ducked down where you were. My boy was a toddler then and he was a terror for undressing himself. We'd be picking and the raid would come. The other pickers would say, "All right Alice, I'm picking up his shoes, I've got his vest." and I'd just see this little naked body coming along. And I had to run and get him, because the pilots in the planes would machine gun you. If the baby was in the pram and there was a raid, you ran with the pram and tipped it over in the ditch, so it shielded the baby and they didn't see you. My husband, he'd be ploughing, and my boys used to call out, "Dad! Dad! There's a doodlebug coming!" Because they'd make a noise and you'd just see it go. The boys used to get frightened in case it came near him, you see. You'd just see this big flame and once that flame went out, then it'd land. And explode. They flew ever so low. You could see them. And the V2s were the worst because you never saw them. They just come and you was gone. In our house we had what they call a table shelter, and we all slept underneath that, it's like a big iron table with a bottom, and you slept in that. But you could have a shelter in the garden if you wanted to.

The Italian prisoners of war used to come on our farm helping to do odd jobs. My kids loved them. They used to get a rabbit, kill a rabbit, and they'd cook it over the fire, and my boys used to be down there enjoying themselves with them.

During the war, we always got extra rations, being farm workers. I used to put up some of the soldiers' wives. Then if the soldiers were down for the weekend they used to stay at my place. A lot of fiddling went on in the wartime. We got very friendly with this army cook, he used to bring us cheese, meat, sugar, jam, everything! There was one soldier who stayed with us, he was the most wonderful drawer. He used to sit with my boy on his knee and draw and he could write a letter at the same time! He could write a letter to his wife while he was drawing left handed.

Alice Heskitt

KENT INVADED BY ARMY OF HOP PICKERS

No Shortage Of Food: Butcher's Shop Set Up In Barn

HOP picking is going to be a profitable holiday for thousands of Londoners in the Kent gardens this year.

Picking began on most farms on Wednesday, and expert pickers confidently look forward to earning good money, for on many farms the "tally" is three bushels to the shilling.

And there is a splendid crop and no shortage of pickers.

On some of the bigger farms there will be savings groups and pickers will be encouraged to buy savings stamps when they get their pay.

Most pickers have had their fares paid for them and pickers. who have been evacuated from London, have come from as far away as Blackpool.

GIRLS AS BINMEN

Owing to the shortage of men, girls wearing slacks will this year act as binmen. pulling the hops down from the high wires and placing them near the bins.

In many gardens, soldiers will help with the picking.

Farms have their own A.R.P. schemes and if there are raids the pickers will shelter in the trenches which have been dug alongside the fields.

One feature of camp life will be missing this year and that is the sing-songs round the camp fire after the day's work is over, for no pickers will be allowed to light outside fires this year. But the Londoners will be able to enjoy themselves in the village inns which have been allowed extra supplies of beer by the brewers.

JUST IN CASE......

Fifty-two years old Mrs. Shepherd, of Jamacia Road, Bermondsey. mother of a family of ten children, who first came to the Kent hop gardens when she was six weeks old, and has only missed one hopping since, is safely installed with her belongings in her hut at Whitbread's Farm. Beltring. near Paddock Wood.

Soon after arrival the bed had been made. curtains put up at the windows, and paper on the shelves, and the family was already settled in for their three weeks' stay in Kent.

When a reporter called they had just finished their dinner off the piece of beef which they had brought down from London, and the hut was well stocked with tinned and other food.

"Just in case we run short," said Pa Shepherd.

when pickers were machine gunned in the fields, farms were bombed and it became almost a daily occurrence for a German airman to land in a hop garden.

But it would take more than that to deter pickers like Mrs. Durant of Plumstead, whose 19-year-old son, Charles, an A.R.P. Warden, has just been commended by the King for rescuing two women trapped in a bombed building.

"We certainly went through something last year that we shall never forget, but our boys have got the better of them and we shall have a peaceful hop picking this year," said Mrs. Durant.

NO SCARING MRS FOSTER

"They won't put me off neither," chuckled Mrs. Foster, of Jamacia Road, South Bermondsey, who is 78 and has 60 visits to the hop fields to her credit.

Monday and Tuesday saw the arrival of the army of pickers — from London. Preliminary arrangements for their arrival had been made by strong advance guards during a busy week-end of preparation.

They came, most of them, by rail in the series of "specials" arranged for their conveyance. The proportion of "invaders" travelling by road was this year necessarily limited in the interests of petrol economy and in consequence, unusually heavy demands were made upon the bus services between rail-head points and the gardens to which the groups of pickers had been allocated.

QUITE LIKE OLD TIMES

Tonbridge, especially, in the early days of the week, presented unprecedented scenes of activity. Crowds of Londoners swarmed from the station, with the arrival of each train, weighed down with unbelievably bulky quantities of kit. Children, even the toddlers, did their share of the carrying. Some of them seemed almost to be obliterated by the volume of luggage under which they struggled. Standing regulations were temporarily relaxed by the bus authorities in the general desire to disperse the vast crowds of arrivals.

HAPPY COCKNEYS

And the most remarkable feature of the influx was that those big. bustling throngs of typical East End Londoners showed no outward and visible signs of their ordeals during the winter. They were the good-natured laughing crowds that were familiar during the hopping festivals of peace days.

This year, food rationing has presented new problems in accommodating our huge family of guests. The Ministry of Food, however, for weeks past has been getting the feeding machinery in motion so that all was in

Kent Messenger, 5th September 1941

99

EVEN HOP-PICKERS WERE BOMBED.—Clearing away the debris after a bomb had fallen near some hoppers' huts in a Kent hop garden.

AGRICULTURAL LEAVE FOR HOPPING

When I was in the army, I happened to go down one weekend to the old farm where we went hopping, and the farmer there was a very nice chap, very friendly. So he said, "Where are you stationed Mick?" I told him. So he said, "I'll get you twenty-eight days agricultural leave." So I said, "That sounds a good idea." Went back, got a letter, "You've got twenty-eight days agricultural leave for Lily Farm, Paddock Wood." "Right." So I got the leave and went down there, hop-picking, plum pulling, whatever. And after the time was up, and I should go back to the army, he said, "Don't go back, I've got another twenty-eight days extension for you." Nice fellow, old Claude. That was wartime.

Some of those farmers who had their men in the army, they got them leaves to do the harvest, apple-picking, plums, hop-picking, tractor driving, anything. One year I remember I went back there, and he said, "Oh I don't want you on Lily Farm this hopping." I said, "Why what's the matter?" "I want you to come over to our other farm, Church Farm." – that's his brother's farm up the road a bit. So he said, "You'll like it over there." So I said, "Well, yes." So a big blonde lady was over there, she was an instructor from the RAF, she worked as a pole puller. A women pole puller! Bur-bur, they called her!

This particular farm we was on, one Sunday morning there was about seven, eight of us, walking back to the farm. As we're walking near the farm, we heard a siren go at Paddock Wood, and we see all the German bombers going over, swarms of them. And all of a sudden one of them must have took fright and said, "Oh I'm turning back." It's turned back and come towards the farm and dropped this stick of bombs. We heard them screaming down, "Cor, bombs!" So we dived into the bleedin' hedge, eight bombs went right across the bleedin' farm.

The kids were all in the huts, so me and my brother-in-law got up and ran down to the farm. They were all in the huts, the women and kids, screaming, "Mum! Where's dad?" The first bomb was in the orchard. Blew up apple trees and did a lot of damage. Next one landed in the hop field, and made a big hole – unexploded it was. So me and my brothers looked at that, "Cor, look how it's gone through that ground. Like a knife in butter." Little did we know that any minute, if it had blown up we would have gone up with it. Then we went up a bit further, where the hop bins were, about four bits blew up in the air then. Had it been a weekday we would have all been killed. Then we found another couple of bombs further over at the railway line.

Anyway, the police came down. Then the army came down. They said, "Right. You've got to be evacuated.

Can't do hops no more on this farm." So the farmer took us to the Church Farm, his brother's farm. When we got there, there's no room to sleep, no place for us. We said, "What are we going to do?" He said, "Well the only place is that barn over there. Some get in the barn or the cow shed, there are no cows there, so make some room there." And they all got in wherever they could. We went in the barn, about four other families in this barn. Just an old barn, straw and everything. And we stayed there until the hopping had ended.

While we were there, they said, "Can't go on Lily Farm no more, it's out of bounds." Next thing we knew, we're sent back to the farm to pick the hops while the unexploded bombs are still there. One day we were out there picking, when an army lorry came along. "What do they want?" Two soldiers got out. "Got unexploded bombs here?" "Yes, one up there, one there and two over there." So they said, "Get right back in the ditches. We're going to explode them." And they got out fuse wires or something, "Stand clear." Bang! Up they went. First they'd said we couldn't go there picking so we'd all had to go up to Church Farm, and then we was picking there at Lily farm and all the time while the bombs were there!

Mike Fitzgerald

PRISONERS OF WAR

There had been a fair bit of bombing where we used to go hop-picking. You could see where the bomb had actually dropped right near the huts and made a crater. We used to have a fire in that crater later on, and tell ghost stories round it. Also there was a prisoner of war camp fairly near by and my nan had all things that the prisoners had made from wood bark and handed over to us, things like owls that they'd carved out. I think they must have been on good terms with the POWs. Even though they all had sons fighting in the war. Even my dad, when the grandchildren asked him about the war, did he shoot anyone, he always said that what you've got to remember is that the German soldiers didn't want to be involved any more than he did.

Elaine Jones

Cattle Machine-Gunned

Enemy air activity again developed over this same area late morning on Sunday, and bombs were dropped, but no damage was done.

* * * *

During this raid a German 'plane was shot down over the rural district and crashed in a cobnut plantation, burying itself with its pilot, deep in the ground.

As this 'plane had passed over the adjacent parish a large herd of cows in a field near the Pilgrims' Way were machine-gunned, but none was hit.

Wartime hop-pickers with sandbags in the background

A VANISHED WORLD

1965 Fisher's Farm, Albert Bowers on the "Crow's nest"

THE COMING OF THE MACHINES

Changing over to the machines took the atmosphere out of hopping. After the machines came, there was no family atmosphere. Before, when you had sacking and bins, and everybody had them in rows, you'd pull your bines down and you'd stand there picking them, and we'd all shout out telling one another jokes or start singing. Someone would start singing and then everybody'd be singing ... and then they done away with the bins and they started the machine picking and it was like you were in a factory. They'd go out and cut the hops down, then hook them onto great big hooks, and we'd all be standing in a row at the machines, either side. They'd go round and strip the bines, then you'd got to sort the leaves out ... like being in a factory.

People still go down because they've been going for generations haven't they? They don't just go down for the hopping do they? They meet their mates from years ago. You don't see them people from one hopping to another but they're family friends. Some come from Hammersmith, Stepney and Poplar – all over. I don't think they do it for the money any more, you couldn't earn that much. They had that song didn't they? "When you go to go hopping, earn a bob or two."

Tom Easterbrook

Everyone was unhappy because the hand picking stopped. We did know it was going to stop. There was a lot of talk previously about it. There'd been talk for a couple of years about these machines being brought in. But the machines didn't do the job as well as the people.

My boy cried when hop-picking finished and they got machines in. They told us that it was our last year. What picking there was left, the homedwellers could do. Chrissy cried when he knew he wasn't going the next year. Well, he had a good time, didn't he? He liked it, because he had made friends with kids from everywhere on the farm.

Ellen Russell

After the flood at Whitbread's in 1968, the hop-picking really tailed off all together. Then the machines came in ... well, all mechanised things have been resented through the ages. I don't think there were protests; there may have been a few odd ones. But it was accepted. I think that flood put the kibosh on it all. I don't think anybody cared so much after that. A complete way of life had finished. I would love it to come back. My son Michael still says now, "I wish I could buy a hop field and put some huts in it. I think people would pay me to come and do it." I said, "I'm sure they would. A lot of them would." All regret that passing. It was a carefree, happy way of life. A different way of life for us. You found only the poor people went. I think the companionship, the utter difference in the way of life, being out in the open, fresh air. A happy family way of life with everybody sharing – well they did anyway in those days. You didn't have to leave the children and go out to work in a factory or anything like that. You could take them with you. You lived rent free in the huts. I think a lot of people were very glad to earn those extra shillings. It was the machines that spoiled it all. That's progress isn't it? Or is it? Who knows.

I think they started to employ the machines very slowly, while the pickers were still there. Some had been brought in. Maybe they might finish the hop-picking after three weeks and then let the machines do the rest. Which wouldn't be very much left. I don't think they really took over until that flood. When there's a so-called improvement they all think they have got to do it as well. One started with machines and the others felt they had to do the same. Competition. I think a lot of the smaller ones still did keep their pickers.

Maybe as long as ten years ago, I went to a place where the farmer had died, but he'd left it in his will that the hop huts in the orchard should be left standing and the people that had used them all those years could go there and have a holiday.

Kathleen Ash

Mrs Withers returns to the hop farm 1966

If hop-picking was still going on I'd still be going. It's one of those things that draws you back each year. I used to look forward to it. When it finished, I used to go down now and again at weekends just for the day, out of nostalgia really.

Flo Batley

I do remember the machines coming in. Certain farms were mechanised all of a sudden, or they just finished with the hops completely and went over to something else. People did go to work on the machines even when I was there, but I don't think people liked it. I suppose you accepted what authority put before you. I don't think there was a lot of questioning, especially because it was women. It wasn't like a trade union, it was mostly women – because the men only came at weekends.

I've seen the machines at work. They come round and tear all the hops down. The work was all inside. There wasn't that open air thing about it. And there was the noise. Whereas the hop field was very peaceful, I mean it was so quiet. You'd just hear other people chattering, and then a whistle blowing for the break. It was lovely.

We should have stopped when our farm went completely mechanised. But my grandmother was ill with cancer, and she just wanted to go hop-picking, so we chased round and found a farm where they were still picking, a Whitbread farm it was. They said we could go as long as we could find four pole pullers, because they were short on pole pullers, which were the men who helped take the bines down. So my brother and his friends were recruited just so that she could go hop-picking. And that's how much it meant to her. It's amazing, but we were all ready to pull out all the stops to see if she could at least do that for the last time.

Elaine Jones

1949 Mrs Withers and family "at the bin"

Kent Messenger 1933

My mum gave up hop-picking when it all turned to machinery and they put all the Londoners off, they just had their own pickers, people that lived there. That's what really broke Mum up, when it finished. She used to look forward to it so much. Well, it was company, all the different people. My mum was a good picker and everybody knew her down there. And they were all of the same sort. You know, there was no high and mighty people, or anything like that. They all mucked in together and shared everything. If somebody never had anything, there was always somebody there to help them out. Not like nowadays. If anybody was ill, they did what they could for them. It was a different way of life.

Florence Burgess

My mother was most upset when they switched over from hand picking to machines ... She must have been nearly seventy. And then one year they sent to say they didn't need them any more, though they knew the previous year they were going over to machines. They wrote to say they didn't need pickers because the machines had been installed and that was the end. But even then, my parents went down at weekends during the season. One of the people who used to go hop-picking with my parents still goes down there. The farmer lets them use the hop huts. Some of the wives now work in the kilns. When the machines take the hops into the kiln, they pick the leaves out because the machines pick the whole bine. They have women to pick the leaves out. People still want to go down there. It was their life.

Eileen O'Sullivan

The year before we started hop-picking, it was done by hand. But the next year, they had the machines in. People didn't like the machines. They still had to pick the leaves out, same as doing bin picking but it was inside. I never went inside, I got to drive the tractor. Each side you had the hops and you'd go through the middle with the tractor, I'd stand up on the crow's nest ... which was attached to the wagon ... like a big frame with a platform on top. You'd stand up there and cut the hops as you went through. Cut them from the top, with someone cutting from the bottom and then a woman would come along and pick them up and put them on the back of a lorry. Then you'd take them to the shed where they'd go through the machine and get shredded. As they came through the other side, the women used to be there picking all the leaves out. It wasn't as good as bin picking.

Albert Bowers

I think we went about twenty years before they started the machines. My mum reckoned hop-picking was good for you – set you up for the winter – she got well in with this farmer so she could go down to his farm every year. In 1959, my mum never went down hopping and she died that Christmas.

Vi Lewis

Minnie Martin

1953 Elaine Jones (Centre), brother John, mother and grandparents

GOING BACK

When I was married I went to Paddock Wood. It was a lovely place. There were brick huts just like bungalows. It had all been upgraded by the time I got married. When I was at Paddock Wood my family were all married – my brothers and sisters that is – they all loved hop-picking but they couldn't be bothered to take all the stuff down. I was the only one who used to go hop-picking and I used to have two or three huts and they'd all have their holidays down there, but they would come out picking.

My children weren't too keen on hop-picking. I only took them a couple of years. They didn't like the picking. It makes your hands all black, so they never liked eating food after hop-picking. The black came from the stuff you spray the hops with. They used the same stuff when I was a child. My mum used to take all the old clothes up to the fields and you used to have your sandwiches in them if you were fussy. If you were hungry you weren't fussy, you just ate what was there. It makes you smell as well but I love the smell of hops.

I was a bit disappointed when my children weren't interested in hop-picking, plus hand-picking was beginning to be phased out. This was when the machine picking came in. In the end of hop-picking younger people were going and taking caravans and that down and using it as a holiday base and they wouldn't go out and pick the hops. So that's when they stopped the hop-picking – stopped people going down and they got machines in.

Kit O'Connell

HOPPING HOLIDAY Evn Standard 17 8 64

ABOUT 10,000 Londoners from Bow, Stepney, Bermondsey and Rotherhithe are preparing for their annual September holiday in the Kent hopfields.

They are a vanishing race; hop - picking machines increase in number each year and this autumn it is estimated that at least 70 per cent of the crop will be machine-picked.

Before the last war, the number of Londoners clearing the bines would have been closer to 30,000.

It used to be possible for an East-End family to have a holiday picking hops and also return home with £20 or £30 in their pockets. But things have changed since then and most pickers settle for just a working holiday paid for by the hops.

Philip Howard looks at London

TIMES. 4/10/72

Mechanical fingers pick a tradition almost bare

The traditional cheap holiday for Londoners has just ended, now that the hops in Kent and Sussex have been picked. A century ago a supercilious spectator described the autumn migration from the East End to the hop gardens : "The last ingathering of autumn that finds employment for the poor . . . we see them travelling to the hop grounds with baby on back, and leading children by the hand, carrying cradle and bed, saucepan and kettle, and no doubt nearly everything their humble home contains."

Today almost all the hops in Britain are picked by mechanical fingers ; but a few human pickers from London are still needed, vestigial survivors of the great annual army. For instance, Mr Peter Tipples, whose family has been growing hops in the wealds of Kent for three generations, and probably longer if he was interested in genealogy, employed six families from London this year.

The men helped to cut the bines into the hop-picking carts ; the women picked stray leaves out of the hops on the moving belts in the machine shed.

His families still come from the old hop-picking parts of London, and the women still customarily make the arrangements, writing in April to book their usual hut for September. They live in a wing of the old hopper huts, cooking over logs on the big central brick fireplaces.

Rows of disused huts as cramped as Trappist cells stand empty, or are used for storing apple boxes, witnesses of the great autumn camp of the old days. Mr Tipples's family firm is one of the big growers, farming between 80 and 90 acres of hops. When he started work as a tallyman in one of his hop gardens before the last war it employed 120 families a year.

He still has files of letters from housewives in Wapping and Stepney booking their bins for the picking, or insisting that on no account should they be given hut 25 this year.

His job included rattling on the doors to rouse the encampment at 6.30 am, and measuring the hops from the bins into baskets, through a running spray of argument about the way he was pressing the hops down in the basket, the miserable pea-like size of the cones, and the amount of leaves that had been picked.

In those days he paid a shilling for five bushels of hops; a first-class woman could pick between 25 and 30 bushels a day. He still has the printed cards he used to send out, telling the

Londoners to catch the special, cheap hop-pickers' trains at 5.50 am from London Bridge and New Cross; and reminding them to bring their national insurance cards and cooking utensils. He met them with horse and cart at the station.

Three times a week he organized a "sub night" to advance the pickers money against their final earnings; and on Saturdays he ran an apple scramble for the children in the hop gardens driving a lorry through them and tipping small apples off the back.

The village grocer set up shop in the camp for the duration. Altogether, Mr Tipples's memory of the great London hop-picking days makes them sound a merry time of cider, and cockney song and sunburnt mirth.

There were organizational problems with ration cards and transport during the war; and once there was a strike for more money. But Mr Tipples was far enough ahead with the picking to be able to afford to cut off the water and the ration of two faggots of wood to each hut a day.

After three days he broke the strike by picking out the "ringleaders" and personally putting them on the train. In September, 1940, no pickers turned up for the harvest, because rumour had run through London that the Luftwaffe was machine-gunning the Kent hop gardens three times a day. Then the Germans started to bomb London and suddenly there were more pickers than he could employ.

Mr Tipples has happy memories of his Londoners, and thinks that they were content with him. Otherwise why should some families have gone back to him year after year for 50 years ? He mechanized quite early, about 12 years ago, not because he thought machines would do the job more cheaply but because his pickers were fading away. Those who did come told him about their summer holidays in Spain.

He says: "Nothing could ever do the job as well as the best pickers. Some women could fill their bins with hops picked singly and without a leaf. But the average sample by machine is better than the average picking by hand."

The Londoners who still go hop-picking in Kent are heirs and heiresses of a very old custom that will probably survive as long as there are hops in beer. Today they use their hopper huts as country cottages, coming down to camp in them at weekends and Bank holidays outside the picking season.

AN ENDURING MEMORY

We'll never forget our hopping days. My daughter took us to Whitbread's a few weeks ago, which we thoroughly enjoyed. In two weeks, all our family, our son, two daughters, sister, several grandchildren and great grandchildren are going all around the hop fields again. We always go to Goudhurst, visit the church, sign our names in the visitors' book, and look for our names which I carved on the perimeter wall in about 1936.

Tom Baldwin

Picking hops was one of the most boring and tedious experiences of my life. The bins of hops seemed to be endless. I would volunteer to leave the fields early and get the fires going – occasionally managing to scrounge a few lumps of coal from the train drivers as we picked near the railway line. However, on reflection, I *would* consider these to be happy times of close-knit family life and neighbours who were pleased to share.

After working in the fields all day, the favourite pastimes were stealing the local farmer's fruit, playing football or rounders in the community field with the mums and dads, sing-songs around the bonfire or visits to the local pubs.

This is what the people looked forward to as their annual break and most of them thoroughly enjoyed it, returning year after year. After many years, I returned to our old hop farm. The farm was derelict and I could not recognise it as the place of so much noisy activity that it was in the 1940s.

Tony Whytock

Lovely it was. And everybody who went says the same thing. It was an opportunity to meet all the family. To all be together at the same time. It was magical really. You'd light a fire in the evening, and tell ghost stories. Sing all songs round the fire, sit there talking and jawing, telling tales.

You can't explain the feeling. When we meet with Billy and everybody, he cries not coming. And he cries that they'll never get times like that again. No matter what you done or where you went. It was just like a wonderland. It's like that feeling when you're a little kid Christmas eve; that lovely, wonderful ... that's what hopping was like. It was just fantastic.

We're always talking about having a reunion, but we're such a big family. And there's so many and you have children and their wives, and their children; there's so many they can't all get in anyone's place. So my cousin Billy said they're all going to come over and have a chat one night. And we're all going down there because our farm used to have a white gate, and we used to sit on that, and you could walk that way to The Cow, and that way to the other pub. We didn't used to drink, but the pub was a meeting place. We used to get dressed up and we'd walk from our white gate to The Cow, couple of miles wasn't it? And we want to do that, all of us my age group. Our ambition is to all be together and walk from the white gate to The Cow and back. Just to recapture that feeling.

Anne Fitzgerald

The pond and the oast house remembered (photo lent by John Wardley)

When you were hop-picking, you had a lot of freedom. I was in service, always at someone's beck and call, so it was "do this", "do that", and "don't do this" and "don't do that". Well down there, hop-picking, if Mum told you to do anything, you'd go and hide for five minutes, so she couldn't find you! It was good.

The last time we ever went down hop-picking, it was in 1947. I went down with my friend and we stayed in this hut together with our children. When I talk about that time to my daughter Eileen, I say to her, "Can you remember anything about hop-picking?" What she remembers was that I didn't have a mat when I went down to the hop fields. So I pinched – not pinched, *borrowed* – one of the sacks from the hop fields and put it on the floor inside the hut to make a mat for us. Of course, Mr Dawes came round one day, "I'm looking for these sacks!" My daughter says she can remember me saying to her: "Go and take this sack and chuck it round the back of the huts!" If old Dawes had found us with it in the hut he'd have made us pay a fine for it, or maybe he'd even have sent us off the hop field!

Laura Murphy

We went down a couple of years ago to the farm we used to pick on – just to have a look round. There's no huts left there. The oast house is converted to flats. The Mill Pond Farm is a pottery now. It's all changed, nothing like we remembered. We went up the path where the hop field used to be, and it's all disused now. The spring where we used to go and get our drinking water was so pure, you couldn't drink a purer water. A little spring running out the side of the chalk hills ... it's dried up now!

Albert Bowers

Fisher's Farm, that was a lovely little farm that. You went down a little lane about two hundred yards, turn right and you were out of this world! There was a great big pond with a couple of ducks on it next to the oast house. Then just round the corner was the hopping huts. That was a lovely little farm.

Tom Easterbrook

The old hop huts (photo lent by Joe Creamer)

IN PERPETUITY

When the farmer at Sutton Valence died, he left the huts to the people to be used forever, and people who used to pick there still go down there for holidays. They have to stay away during the hopping season, because they've got new people come there who work the machines and that. It was very nice of the farmer to do that. We went down there last year and saw the people down there who used to go, and there was one woman of ninety-two who was in the hut there, and my son knew of her relatives, and spoke to her, and she still goes down there every year and has her holiday down there.

When my wife died, she was cremated and we took the ashes down to the part of the farm where she used to be and we spread the ashes there, with some wild flowers. We go down there on the anniversary of her death, and see all the wild flowers growing on it. Unfortunately they've shifted the gates, and now there are cars and roads there. It hadn't been touched for hundreds of years before that. Anyway, we've put some flowers for my wife over the other side of the road and we're waiting for them to grow.

Harry Demarne

CONTINUING LINKS WITH KENT

The farm closed down thirty years ago. The lady still lives on the farm, made one of the oast houses into a house. She loved hopping. She said she'd love to get a hopping reunion up, where all the hoppers go and pick for the day. Big charity thing.

My eldest brother bought this small holding down at Five Oak Green, near Paddock Wood. And they built huts, had old wooden huts they put on there. And it stood like that for years and years, they used to go down week after week, month after month, they loved it, he and his wife. Anyway he died last year, August before, and his son took over. So he decided to chuck all the old stuff and build a bungalow. So he took all the old huts down and knocked it all down. And he built a lovely bungalow.

Mike Fitzgerald

I moved in 1957 to where I live now. I went to Whitbread's again for another year, but my eldest son was at a Central school and by then the authorities had clamped down a little bit. You could take them away for about a fortnight, but you couldn't keep them away from school. I lost my husband in 1962. Some time after that I went to a place near Benenden, in Kent. It was a tiny little farm owned by two spinster sisters and a brother. They had this hop farm. My neighbour who'd been picking there for some time said, "Would you like to go there?" And we said we'd go. It was the most primitive place I'd ever been. It was just a wooden hut. Nothing there, no hot water or anything, you started from scratch. But it was fun and it made a holiday.

The dear old brother was such a nice man, just like somebody you see on the television; a few tufts of white hair and a battered old hat. And he was the one that kept the oast house going – where they roast the hops. The two sisters used to wear those caps and long dresses. They had another sister that was married and she was their bookie. But the two sisters used to do the measuring, they were lovely. They lived in this farmhouse. The kitchen was really big and had a huge open fire, where they used to cook. It had an oven in the wall, and a big iron bar where they could hang pots. They had a stone sink in the corner and a well – they had a well in their kitchen! They said that the house was built in the time of the Huguenots. There was a secret room between some of the rooms. I only went hop-picking there one year. The following year the brother died, and they decided not to carry on – it was too much for them, I think. I kept in contact with them for several years just with Christmas cards and one year I went back down for a visit. But eventually it tailed off from there. Whether they died or whether they sold the farm or whether they moved away, I don't know. So that was the end of my hop-picking. I didn't go any more after that because I had to keep at work.

Kathleen Ash

THE END OF AN ERA

I'd love to go down hopping again, in the old way, not like today. They use machines now. We went to this farm and they took us round and showed us how they do things. But it was all so commercialised. Nothing but machines. You could see that it had all gone. We knew that it was an age that had passed. They were getting rid of all the hoppers. We used to watch for the first week of September. We used to go out the street door, "Got your ticket yet?" they used to say. "Yes, got me ticket this morning, we're off Friday." "Oh, we'll get ours soon." And when they got the letters saying that they wouldn't be needed anymore, women were crying openly, they were really heartbroken. Right at the very last, they kept a few of the homedwellers on, to finish off the last hop-picking. Once that was finished, you knew that it was gone – the end of an era. It was something that would never happen again. They'll never grow again – well they *will* grow again, but they're not there for us. They'll be ripped up and stored away in that shed in no time. We've lost all that.

Charlotte Fowler

Hop-pickers at Paddock Wood station (photo lent by Whitbread Hop Farm)

EPITAPH

They were lovely days down in Kent, especially to get away from our father who was always drunk and very violent to my mum. We knew that by picking my mum was going to get lots of money and be able to clear all her debts. Then we'd go home in new clothes, we'd had a good feed up of food and we'd take a lot of food home with us. We had a lot of fresh air too. It was beautiful. My brother lives in Canada and every time he comes home about every two years that's the first place he goes, down Kent. I say that if you've not been hop-picking, you've not lived.

Kit O'Connell

(photo lent by John Wardley)

When we go down hopping, hopping down in Kent,
See old mother Riley putting up her tent,
With a teio, teio, teio.

Sunday is our washing day, wash things nice and clean;
Boil them in the hopping pot and hang them on the green,
With a teio, teio, teio.

Some say hopping's lousy: don't believe it's true;
We only go down hopping to earn a quid or two,
With a teio, teio, teio.

Hopping is all over, money is all spent,
Wish I never went hopping down in Kent,
With a teio, teio, teio.

AGE EXCHANGE REMINISCENCE BOOKS

The Age Exchange is a theatre and publishing company working with London pensioners on shows and books which record their life experience and their current concerns.

It is a feature of all these books that the contributions come from many pensioners, are lively and easy to read, conversational in style, and lavishly illustrated with photographs and line drawings of the time. All the stories are told in the original words, from transcribed tapes, or pensioners' written contributions.

The following books are already available:

"FIFTY YEARS AGO": Memories of the 1930s, a collage of stories and photographs of day-to-day life around 1933. £2.95

"GOOD MORNING CHILDREN": Schooldays in the 1920s and 30s. Fascinating reading and delightful photographs for today's and yesterday's school children. £3.95

"WHAT DID YOU DO IN THE WAR, MUM?" This book of memories, photos and line drawings provides a clear picture of the wide range of jobs which opened up for women in the war years, and of their undoubted skill and ability in these new areas. These individual stories, full of detail and humour, project a positive image of women as flexible and resilient workers. £3.95

"A PLACE TO STAY": memories of pensioners from many lands. Ethnic elders from the Caribbean, the Asian sub-continent, the Far East, Cyprus and Poland tell of their arrival in Britain and their experience of growing old here. The stories are told in English and in the mother tongues. £3.95

"ALL OUR CHRISTMASES": a book of Christmas memories by London pensioners. £2.95

"MY FIRST JOB": Pensioners' memories of starting work in the 1920s and 30s. £2.95

"CAN WE AFFORD THE DOCTOR?" was a frequent cry before the days of the NHS. This book examines health and social welfare in the early part of this century when people often had to rely on their own resources and remedies to cope with illness or disability. Childhood diseases, infectious diseases, accidents and more serious illnesses are recalled. Doctors and nurses remember their early years of service and conditions in homes and hospitals. The book has many photographs and illustrations. £3.95

"MANY HAPPY RETIREMENTS". "For anyone who has sat through conventional pre-retirement courses, being lectured at by experts, relief is at hand. Wisely used, the refreshing new source material in this lovely book from Age Exchange, with its case studies, transcripts and dramatised cameos, is guaranteed to revitalise even the dullest course." Michael Pilch, Vice President, Pre-Retirement Association. £3.95

"THE TIME OF OUR LIVES", is a compilation of memories of leisure time in the 1920s and 30s. Spare time was limited and money always in short supply, but the stories reveal the energy and enterprise of young people who made thier own entertainment in the days before television. Pensioners who are now in their seventies recall vividly the comedy of their courting days, the dance, cinema, rambling, cycling and outings of their youth. Generously illustrated with photographs and line drawings, this makes good reading for all ages. £3.95

"ON THE RIVER": The recollections of older Londoners who have lived by and worked on the River Thames. Their stories recapture the sense of bustle and industry when the river was London's main thorough-fare and the docks were a crucial source of livelihood for thousands of families. The book contains over 100 full page photographs of the river in its heyday. £12.95 (Hardback)

"GOODNIGHT CHILDREN EVERYWHERE": A remarkable collection of first hand experiences of evacuation in the Second World War. The contributors speak honestly, in many cases for the first time, about the upheaval they went through as children, illustrating their stories with letters they wrote at the time and the photos of themselves which were taken to send home to their parents. Over 250 superb photographs. £15.95 (hardback) £9.95 (softback)

"WHEN WE WERE YOUNG": A delightful anthology of photographs and memories of growing up in the West Country. A record of Age Exchange's South Somerset project in five villages, with reflections on the process from pensioners, staff and children, this book also provides a useful working model for other reminiscence projects. £3.95

"LIVING THROUGH THE BLITZ": Londoners' memories of broken nights in and out of the shelter, being bombed out, hazardous journeys to work, queuing for rationed food, and hunting for shrapnel among the ruins. £4.95

"JUST LIKE THE COUNTRY": The story of families who moved from inner city tenement blocks to the new cottage estates of outer London in the inter-war period. They talk of the challenge involved in making a new life in their "homes fit for heroes", and the sense of nostalgia they felt for the old ways and communities they had left behind. £6.95

THERE ARE SPECIAL PRICES FOR O.A.Ps who wish to order any or all of these books. In all cases postage and packing is extra.

If you would like to order any of the above titles please write to Age Exchange, 11 Blackheath Village, London SE3 9LA. If readers are interested in hiring our touring exhibitions of photographs, they should contact us at the above address, or telephone 081 318 9105.

Printed by: Direct Design (Bournemouth) Ltd., 3 The Courtyard, Thrush Road, Poole, Dorset, BH12 4NP